JOURNEY BACK FROM VIETNAM

One Soldier's Long Road Home From War

JOURNEY BACK FROM VIETNAM

One Soldier's Long Road Home From War

Hòa Bình (Peace)

Wayne Purinton

Specialist Fourth Class Wayne Purinton US Army 1966 - 1968

Langdon Street Press | Minneapolis

OUR NATION REMEMBERS
THE COURAGE, SACRIFICE,
AND DEVOTION TO DUTY
AND COUNTRY OF ITS
VIETNAM VETERANS

DEDICATED TO

SP5 Lee Roger Danielson, U.S. Army
and his family

1st Lt Winfield Wesley Beck, U.S. Army
and his family

Specialist Fifth Class Lee Roger Danielson,
C Company 5th Battalion, 7th Cavalry, First Cavalry Division, U.S. Army,
was born on 1 October, 1947.
He was killed in action in Quang Nam Province, Vietnam, 12 January 1968.
His name is inscribed on the Vietnam Veterans Memorial
in Washington DC on the east wall, panel 34, line 35.

First Lieutenant Winfield Wesley Beck,
C Company 5th Battalion, 7th Cavalry, First Cavalry Division, U.S. Army,
was born 25 October 1942.
He was killed in action in Thua Thien Province, Vietnam, 13 February 1968.
His name is inscribed on the Vietnam Veterans Memorial
in Washington DC on the east wall, panel 39, line 17.

TABLE OF CONTENTS

PREFACE

Wayne's Vietnam Experience and a Friend's Perspective

Wayne Purinton has been my closest personal friend since 1961, so what I am writing is not free of bias. However, because I knew him well before and after his Vietnam experience, I feel I have a unique perspective of the war's impact on him. As you read his book, these observations may provide some insight into Wayne's Vietnam experience.

Wayne Purinton and I first met in the summer of 1961 when Leonard and Irene Purinton drove their four boys to town (WaKeeney, Kansas) from their farm (twenty-five miles from town) to play little league baseball. Wayne, the oldest of the four boys, and I began high school that fall. For four years we played baseball and football, went pheasant hunting at his parent's farm, cruised Main Street endlessly, and attended dances at the VFW Hall in WaKeeney and the Zeman Dance Hall in Collyer, Kansas. I liked Wayne not only because we shared so many common interests, but because he was a kind and thoughtful person who was a great listener.

When we graduated from Trego Community High School in May of 1965, the Vietnam War was heating up. How to avoid getting drafted and speculating on how long "The War" would last was on everyone's mind. Wayne went to Denver to a business school while I began college at Fort Hays State University. We kept in contact and maintained our tradition of hunting pheasants on the opening day of the season at the Purinton farm. Through our conversations, I could tell he was not satisfied with his Denver experience, but I was very surprised and concerned when he announced that he had volunteered for the draft.

When Wayne returned from basic training, he knew he was headed to Vietnam and into harm's way. We had a number of long talks about his uncertain future and while he remained upbeat, it was clear he was under a great deal of stress. After his infantry training at Fort Polk, Louisiana, he returned home before being shipped out to Vietnam. During this visit, we reassured each other that everything would turn out fine, but we both knew he was going to be on the front lines of the conflict. Be cause he feared the worst, we even discussed what I should do if he didn't come back. I was to go to Castle Rock (about a mile from Wayne's home) and talk to him at this beautiful windswept place. The reality of his situation had set in for not only Wayne, but also for his family and friends.

While he was in Vietnam, Wayne and I wrote regularly. His letters described a world of deprivation, destruction, danger, and death as he and his fellow grunts tried to destroy an elusive, determined enemy. My teenage friend who had only killed pheasants and jackrabbits was now killing people and having his comrades killed around him. In addition, he was becoming aware of and troubled by the paradox of the war. He was told and believed the reason he was there was to win the hearts and minds of the South Vietnamese people and ensure their freedom. But how could burning villages, killing livestock, and destroying crops in an effort to defeat the Viet Cong achieve this goal?

When his tour of duty was over, we were relieved and awaited his return home. Wayne had left for Vietnam weighing 140 pounds and in excellent physical condition. When he returned, he weighed just over 110 pounds and was exhausted. While I was shocked by his physical condition, I was more surprised by his reluctance to talk with his best friend about his Vietnam experience. Wayne and I had always shared everything, but now when I asked him about some of the things he wrote to me about, he didn't want to discuss it. I assumed that I was talking to the same kid I had known just a year before, but this was a new Wayne. In time, I let the topic drop for fear of hurting our relationship.

After being discharged from the Army, Wayne attended Dodge City Community College. In addition to completing his Associates Degree, he met the love of his life, Sandy Berends, and got married. With wife and degree in hand, Wayne returned home to begin farming and to raise a family. For twenty years, Wayne did not discuss his Vietnam experiences with me in any meaningful way. I believe that this was because he was consumed with getting his farming operation established and then struggling to save it during the farm crisis of the late 1970s and early 1980s.

In the late 1980s, Wayne, Sandy, and their three children moved to town and his life became more stable and less stressful. Ironically, without the constant stress of the farm, Wayne's war experiences that he repressed for so many years began to surface. In the next few years, Wayne and I would have long talks about the war. He agonized over three particular issues. The first was survivor's guilt. This was especially pronounced around January 12, which is the anniversary of the death of his friend and squad leader, Sergeant Lee Danielson. In a firefight on January 12, 1968, Wayne lay right next to Danielson when he was shot and killed. The second issue involved the death and destruction the war brought to the people of Vietnam, but could not reconcile how the devastation in which he participated could have helped these people. The final issue Wayne struggled with was his faith in his government. How could the government he trusted and the country he was willing to give his life for sacrifice so many in such a dubious conflict?

To deal with these issues, Wayne researched the Vietnam War, traveled to Vietnam and met with his former enemies, and developed an outstanding presentation for high schools and civic groups. Through these efforts, he hoped to get closure and achieve some peace of mind.

However, he finally came to the realization that professional help was necessary when he was diagnosed with Post Traumatic Stress Disorder (PTSD). His treatment for PTSD has helped him deal with its symptoms and to realize these symptoms will persist for the rest of his life.

Today, Wayne Purinton is a grandfather with a full life. He continues to make presentations about his Vietnam experiences to area high schools and civic groups. He is past President of Vietnam Veterans of America Hays, Kansas, Chapter 939. He currently serves as Vice President of the Vietnam Veterans of America Kansas State Council and is Vice President of the Veterans Vietnam Restoration Project Board of Directors.

In May of 2001, he traveled to Cadott, Wisconsin, to visit the grave of Sgt. Danielson and meet the Danielson family. Wayne answered many of the family's questions and provided some long-delayed closure for everyone. He made a third trip to Vietnam in the spring of 2009 to participate in a humanitarian aid mission to help construct a three-room kindergarten school for a rural village. He is still trying to make a difference in the lives of these people and in some way make amends for what he feels was the devastation of this beautiful country.

This book is based on Wayne's letters home that his mother and father saved and discovered in their closet in June 2000. As Wayne began reading his accounts of the war, he began to recall places and events that had long been suppressed. Ironically, his PTSD continues to fog his memory of events even after reading his own accounts. Wayne saw these letters as another opportunity to make a difference and began putting together his book. He traveled to the National Archives and Records Administration in College Park, Maryland, to research the 5th Battalion, 7th Cavalry Staff Journals, or officer's log, to corroborate his accounts of these events.

Wayne's book is not an indictment of the Vietnam War. It is instead a firsthand account of how a Kansas farm boy dealt with and was impacted by the horrors of this war. The letters are simple expressions of the hopes and fears of the average person in such an environment. We rightly glorify the actions of war heroes, but seldom do we take a careful look at the average soldier doing his duty and trying to stay alive while in harm's way. Wayne's letters home provide a window into the world of the average soldier in combat. Wayne helps us understand that war wounds soldiers both physically and psychologically, and, therefore, when our country asks for their sacrifice, we must be prepared to treat both types of wounds upon their return.

Dan Deines Ph.D. CPA
Ralph Crouch, KPMG Professor of Accounting
Kansas State University

INTRODUCTION

For years I have struggled with my experiences in Vietnam and my return home to a country that did not fully accept my commitment to serve. I knew in my mind that certain incidents I could only vaguely recall or had blocked entirely from my memory had indeed happened. When my letters home from Vietnam surfaced in June of 2000, it was like opening a window to the past. My parents had the insight to save them, and it seems the letters came back into my possession at just the right time.

The death of my squad leader, Lee Danielson, had a profound effect on my life. It just as easily could have been me, rather than Lee. Most days, I fly the American flag to remember and honor a life that was cut short all too soon and to commemorate all who gave their lives defending our great nation.

These letters home from Vietnam have been my motivation to write this book. My hopes are that the book will help other veterans with their own internal conflicts, bring understanding to those who have never been to war, and supplement my educational program for young people regarding the potential realities of military service.

Included in this work are interviews with Ken Baldwin and Father Jim Moster. Ken and I went through basic training, advanced individual training and served together in Vietnam. Father Jim Moster (retired) served as the Chaplain at the Colmery-O'Neal Veterans Administration Medical Center in Topeka, Kansas. Father Jim gave me counsel during my stay at the VA hospital while I was undergoing treatment for Post-Traumatic Stress Disorder.

ACKNOWLEDGMENTS

I would like to give special thanks to the following individuals who have supported and helped me in the writing of this book.

My Wife Sandy

My father and mother, Leonard and Irene

My best friend, Dan Deines

Dianne Tegtmeyer Barnett

Michael J Briggs

Father Jim Moster

Weeden Nichols

Joanne Emerick

Gerhard Brostrom

Karen Cole

Ken Baldwin

Chris Glassman

casualgraphics

Hays, Kansas

AUTHOR'S NOTE

This is a work of nonfiction and readers may assume that the events are true, the characters are real, and the dialogue has been recreated to the best of my recollection. Nothing in life can ever be cleaned completely of fiction, because memory is unreliable and selective at the best of times. To those whom I may have misquoted, misnamed, or mischaracterized, I apologize. I did the best I could with the limited faculties I still possess.

FOREWORD

The greatest resources in the United States are Americans. The greatest Americans are those who voluntarily put themselves in harm's way to serve our country. Wayne's letters home reflect the struggles and sacrifices of those who so honorably serve our nation. Every freedom-loving American should acquaint themselves with their service. As a social science teacher, I believe these experiences are worth much more for students than a teacher's lecture or a reading from the text. Thank you, Wayne, for your service and for making your experiences available to the rest of us with your letters home and your book. We can never repay you and can only hold your experience in the highest esteem.

Keith Rains
Social Science Instructor
Little River High School
Little River, KS

Throughout history, soldiers have gone to war. They have experienced a wealth of emotions and have witnessed destruction and death. They have come home carrying heavy burdens that they were unwilling or unable to share. War changes everyone who serves and affects not just the soldier but his or her family and friends—leaving them to wonder about their loved one's experiences and the changes that have resulted.

Through soldiers' letters, war has been made personal, giving those who read them an understanding of history and, perhaps more importantly, a glimpse into the hearts and souls of the soldiers who lived that history.

Wayne Purinton went to war in Vietnam in 1967. The nineteen-year-old

Kansas farm boy endured it all: countless days of trudging through the jungle, helicopter rides to attack Viet Cong hamlets, endless searches for an enemy that could not be distinguished from a friend, the terror of being caught in an ambush, and the death of his squad leader. Wanting and needing to share, Wayne wrote the details of his experiences to his parents and brothers. But Wayne could not put into words the horrors he witnessed; those who had never been in combat simply would not understand.

Wayne survived the Vietnam War physically, but came home carrying silent images and grief that he kept locked inside for decades. The reemergence of his war letters after thirty-two years has been a source of healing for Wayne and a source of understanding for his family members and friends. Moreover, for his fellow Vietnam veterans, reading Wayne's letters has opened the doors to communicating their own feelings and experiences. Finally, his letters now serve to educate future generations about war through the words of a common soldier.

Joanne Emerick
Instructor of American History

During the early 1990s, a friend of mine who had attended graduate school told me about a class that was being offered at Fort Hays State University to teachers. The class covered the Vietnam era and was offered through the Kansas Department of the Humanities.

I had been talking to our school administration about creating a course that would concentrate on this topic, so the timing was very good. Within weeks of enrolling, information was sent explaining the class and what was expected of class participants A preliminary schedule included with the material showed one morning was to be spent listening to a presentation by a Vietnam Veteran: Wayne Purinton.

That summer was the first time I met Wayne. I remember some points he made during his talk and program, and I also remember thinking that he was a little nervous, which was something I sympathized with. It made me realize how difficult it would be to get up in front of a bunch of strangers—teachers, no less—and present information on a difficult topic that all of us had, to a certain extent, lived through.

I enjoyed Wayne's program enough that when I was able to get a Vietnam-era class added to our schedule, he was one of the first people I contacted about coming to present to my class. He has spoken to students enrolled in that course at Smoky Valley High School each of the past twelve years. During that time, he has spoken on a number of emotionally sensitive subjects concerning his experience in Vietnam and after.

Wayne has opened his life up over the years to my students in a way that has not only been educational, but also very thought-provoking.

Mr. Purinton has tinkered with his program over the years and his addition of the letters he wrote home from Vietnam has been a real eye-opener for our students. In reading these, a person can gain much valuable insight into the thoughts and emotions an American soldier would have dealt with while serving in a combat unit during the Vietnam War.

Wayne's writing is very easy to understand. It has not been edited to make it seem "more refined" or exciting. His letters and his observations are very matter-of-fact in the way they are presented—just the plain and simple truth. It seems the high school students who have seen these appreciate the realism and the truthfulness. In a time when hype is added to everything in our world, Wayne's letters are powerful firsthand teaching tools that focus on the realities of war and its impact on a young Kansas soldier.

Bill Ferguson
Smoky Valley High School
Lindsborg, KS

The Face of Viet Nam

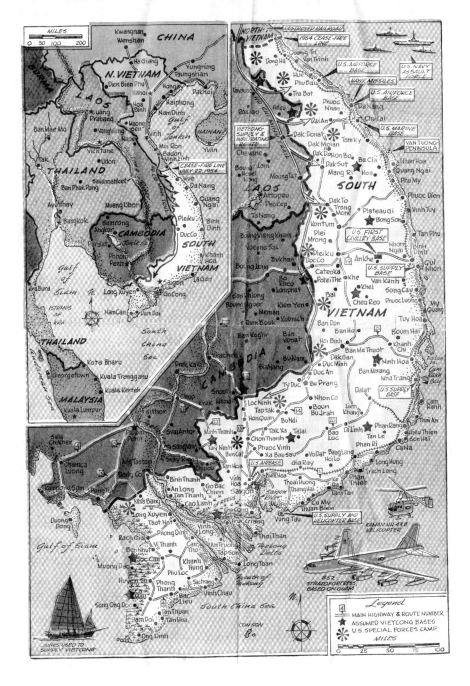

5TH BATTALION 7TH CAVALRY STAFF JOURNALS, OR OFFICER'S LOG

Research of the 5th Battalion, 7th Cavalry Staff Journals or Officer's Log was conducted at the National Archives and Records Administration at College Park, Maryland. These declassified records of radio traffic, officer's action journals, and after-action reports are used to supplement the narrative. They are normally preceded by a military time, a unit, and a location. There is no footnoting or end noting of entries. Readers may contact the author for more information about sources and documentation if they wish.

Note: Underlined text connects the letters home with staff journals or officer's log.

ABBREVIATION INDEX

AO .... Area of Operation
Arty .... Artillery
ARA .... Aerial Rocket Artillery
AW .... Automatic weapon
BN .... Battalion
BS, AT ...... Location
CO .... Commanding Officer
CP .... Command Post
KIA .... Killed In Action
LP .... Listening Post
LZ .... Landing Zone
OCA .... Off-site consequence analysis
OP .... Observation Post
Plts .... Platoons

PZ .... Pick-up Zone
Rds .... Rounds
SA .... Small arms
S-2 .... Intelligence Officer
S-3 .... Operation Officer
SITREP GREEN ....All clear no enemy
TD .... Touch Down
TOC .... Tactical Operation Center
VCS .... Viet Cong Sympathizer
VIC ....Vicinity
WIA .... Wounded In Action
Wpn .... Weapon
XO .... Executive Officer

THE CHIPPEWA HERALD

Chippewa Falls, Wisconsin Sunday, May 27, 2001

By: Mark Gunderman

Survivor still lives with trauma of battle

"I will never forget helping carry his body back to base camp," Wayne Purinton said, recalling the day Lee Danielson of Cadott was killed in Vietnam. Like millions of soldiers before him, he thought it could have been him.

"The date January 12, 1968, a day that I will never forget, started out all right. Late in the afternoon, our platoon was called upon to go help another platoon of Charlie Company. They were pinned down and needed help. Arriving on the scene, our platoon soon came under fire and was also pinned down in locked battle," Purinton recalls.

"I crawled forward to assist Sgt. Danielson. We were lying in a small trench, but were above ground level. About that time, all hell broke loose. A North Vietnamese Army machine gunner began to bear down on our position."

Purinton said he froze in fear. Danielson was hit by the machine gun fire. Eventually Purinton was able to find cover behind a large rock. "Only later, after the action died down, did I realize that Sgt. Danielson had been mortally wounded. As darkness set in, we were able to retrieve his body, then we began to retreat, taking Sgt. Danielson with us," Purinton said.

The next day, Purinton wrote home: "Things have really been going bad lately. My squad leader was killed last night. Four men were killed yesterday. Sure is a bad feeling to see a friend die, as I was lying close to him when he got shot."

He wrote home again about the battle on January 22: "This has been a long hard year and (I) sure will be glad when it's over with, but I think I have learned a lot from it. A battle is something most people read about or watch on TV. I'll never forget January 12, as we really got in a fix. I was caught in the open while enemy machine gun fire was raking the ground. It was really a shock to see my buddy lying there with a hole in his head." [12]

CHAPTER ONE

The Fall of 1966

By the end of 1966, U.S. troop levels had reached 389,000. There were 5,008 Americans killed in action and 30,093 wounded in action. Over half of the American causalities were caused by snipers and small-arms fire during Viet Cong ambushes. Handmade booby traps and mines planted everywhere in the countryside by the Viet Cong also caused American causalities. American allies fighting in Vietnam included 45,000 soldiers from South Korea and 7,000 Australians. There were an estimated 89,000 soldiers from North Vietnam who infiltrated into the South via the Ho Chi Minh trail during 1966. [1]

In the fall of 1966, at the age of nineteen, I was drifting along, not knowing what I wanted to do with my life. I had recently graduated from a business school in Denver and had yet to find a job in my field. I decided to go back home and take a labor job with a construction company. My life was going nowhere fast. Without a student deferment, I was likely to be drafted into the Armed Forces.

One day in September while driving my car, it occurred to me that what I needed to do was enter the military. I reasoned that, following my service, I would be able to start my career. I believed it was an honor and my duty to serve my country, remembering JFK's famous words: "And so my fellow Americans, ask not what your country can do for you; ask what you can do for your country."

Those words played in my head as I drove down to the local draft board to volunteer for service. I was well aware of the many dangers of combat, but I was willing to lay my life down as so many others have in past and present wars, defending the freedoms that all Americans cherish and enjoy today. I wanted my family and country to be proud of me.

On October 10, 1966, I was inducted into the Army and was sent to Fort Leonard Wood, Missouri, for my basic training. Graduating from basic training in December and following a month's leave at home, I traveled by troop train from Kansas City to Fort Polk, Louisiana, for my AIT (Advanced Individual Training). My friend Ken Baldwin from Lawrence, Kansas, and I went through basic training together and were on the same train New Year's Day, 1967, bound for Leesville, Louisiana, the town closest to Fort Polk. Following AIT, Ken and I served together in Vietnam.

Ken Baldwin stated, "The longest train ride ever from Lawrence, Kansas, to Leesville, Louisiana. The whole train passenger car was full of drunken GIs as it was New Year's Day. When we arrived at Fort Polk, we were sent to an area called Tiger Land. This was the training area for troops bound for Vietnam."

January 3, 1967

Fort Polk, LA

Dear Folks and Brothers,

Well, I finally made it down here and this is the last place on earth I wish I were at. Fort Leonard Wood was nice compared to this place. Our barracks are very old and the food is not good either. This place is known as little Vietnam and the company commander told us all of our training was for Vietnam. This first two weeks will be the worst as we get up at 5 a.m. and stop training in between 8 p.m. and 12 p.m. Well, I have very little time to write, so this will be short. Boy that sure was a long ride down here (troop train). It took about 33 hours. I am sending you my address so you can tell the **Western Kansas World** *and have them put my address in the paper.*

Love, Wayne

February 17, 1967

Fort Polk, LA

Dear Folks,

Hi! I sure am sorry I have not written you in so long, but I have really been busy. We fired the M-60 machine gun today. We went through the escape and evasion course Wednesday night. There were nine of us in our squad and five were captured by the VCs. I was one of them. They took us to the POW camp by truck and threw us in a compound. Boy, that was really rough. I ended up getting my shirt ripped off and black and blue marks all over my chest because I would not talk. I finally escaped. We leave for Pearson Ridge on Sunday p.m., come back Friday morning and then we are all done training. Thank goodness. I guess you can expect me home between March 4th to 6th. Well, I got the bad news today. My orders. I am going to be with the 1st Cavalry Division. That is where after the infantry gets involved in a fire fight, they bring the 1st Cavalry right into the middle of the fight by airmobile, that is helicopters. It sure does not sound good by any means, but I have all the faith in the world I will do alright. In other words, I am going to Vietnam. Well, I hope everyone is doing good and well. Please write.

With love,

Wayne

"The escape and evasion course at Fork Polk. As planned, most of us were captured. We were put in a POW camp and were treated real rough. We were forced to play painful games. One of the games was to have a person stand inside of a truck tire holding it up. Then a group of four or five guys had to run and tackle the person holding the tire. If you did not hit them hard enough, then you got to hold the tire.

One of my high school friends drafted with me was Lonnie LeBombard. He was asked to sign some papers and Lonnie, being a smart aleck, said sure. Then he signed with a big X. They tore off his shirt and roughed him up a bit. When we escaped, we got even with them. We put sand in the gas tanks of their generators. They lost power, the lights went out and we escaped." **Ken Baldwin**

DEPARTMENT OF THE ARMY
HEADQUARTERS 1ST CAVALRY DIVISION (AIRMOBILE)
OFFICE OF THE COMMANDING GENERAL
APO SAN FRANCISCO, 96490

AVDACG

8 January 1967

Dear Trooper,

Welcome to the "First Team" and congratulations on your assignment.

You have been selected to join the newest and most versatile outfit of the modern Army. The 1st Air Cavalry Division symbolizes and is typical of our Army's response to challenge. It has proven to be uniquely qualified and equipped to locate and to destroy the enemy. Your division is the unbeatable combination of American technical sophistication and GI guts. It has met, defeated and pursued the enemy from the China Sea coast to the Cambodian border.

As you sew the attached field patch on your uniform, reflect on the combat achievements of those who wore it before you and the great traditions they established for all of us to follow. Tomorrow's battlefields in Vietnam will continue to call for the courage, determination and skill which have been the mark of a "trooper."

I wish you a pleasant trip to Vietnam and look forward to meeting you at Camp Radcliff, An Khe, the home of the "FIRST TEAM" on whose starting line-up your name has already been entered.

JOHN NORTON
Major General, USA
Commanding

CHAPTER TWO

Easter Sunday

March 26, 1967

The day finally arrived; the reality of going off to war in Vietnam was at hand. I awoke early that morning in anticipation of the day ahead. I was very naïve about what war would really be like. I didn't realize how hard it would be to survive a year fighting the Communists in the rice paddies and dense jungles of Southeast Asia. I had no idea how the long-term effects of war would affect my life—what killing another human being or witnessing the deaths of my comrades would do to my soul. I was still an innocent, bright-eyed, teen-aged boy of nineteen.

Later that morning, a clear bright Easter Sunday, I attended church with my family. Following church, my mother cooked a delicious Easter dinner. In the afternoon, my father took me down to the basement of our home, said a few words of encouragement, and gave me a small Bible to carry out in the field. What does a father say to his son about to go off to war? "I am very proud of you, have faith, stay alert, and be careful." What does a mother say to her son about to go off to war? "I love you son, I will keep you in my heart and pray for your safe return." I was feeling brave, yet very scared about going off to war in a strange country about which I knew very little.

In the late afternoon that Easter Sunday, my family and girlfriend drove me to the Hays, Kansas, airport to begin the first leg of the long journey to South Vietnam. It was a tearful time for us all, knowing that I might not come home. During this time period, for many guys, it was like a death sentence to be sent to Vietnam. It was more so if you're MOS (Military Occupational Specialty) was 11B 20, light weapons infantry.

I had tears in my eyes all the way to Denver. It was a gut-wrenching period of my life, not knowing what fate held for me in this war against Communism. By the time I arrived in Oakland, California, I had calmed down and was doing fine. As I stated in my letter home from Fort Polk informing my family I was going to Vietnam, I again felt that although things didn't look that good, "I have all the faith in the world I will do alright."

CHAPTER THREE

The Trip Over

April 2, 1967

Oakland, CA

Dear Folks,

Hi! Well, just a few more hours and I will be on the way over. I am sending my 1ˢᵗ Cavalry field patch, so maybe you can put it by my picture or something. They said it will take 22 ½ hours to fly there, so it will be a long ride. Our first stop will be in Alaska, then Japan, and then somewhere in Vietnam. I will write as soon as I know my address. Well, guess this is all for now.

With Love,

Wayne

April 3, 1967

Oakland, CA

Dear Mom and Dad,

Hi! I am still waiting to be shipped out. I hope tomorrow. I went to San Francisco last night and rode the cable cars and saw Chinatown. I will write more later.

With Love,

Wayne

My Great Aunt Blanche, who lived in Sacramento, came to San Francisco to meet me and show me around town. We had a great evening visiting and touring San Francisco.

April 4, 1967

Mom and Dad,

We are now in Okinawa. So far, we are having a good trip. We stopped in Tokyo, Japan, last night. We will be in Bien Hoa, South Vietnam in a few hours.

Love,

Wayne

Note: The Okinawa Island chain, known in Western writings as the Ryukyu Islands chain, consists of 143 separate islands, but the term usually refers to the seventy-three islands that were under American administration until 1972.[2]

April 4, 1967

Between Okinawa and

Bien Hoa, South Vietnam

Dear Mom and Dad,

We just left Kadena AFB and are three hours from Bien Hoa. We have been flying between 35,000 to 39,000 ft high and about 680 mph. We left Seattle, WA, at about 9 p.m. Sunday night and it took 10 flying hours to Tokyo. When I woke up, it was 12:15 a.m. Tuesday morning, so we gained a day. The first time I saw day light on the whole trip was just before we landed in Okinawa this morning. It is time to eat a hot meal now, so I will finish this after I eat. Well, they served us a real good meal. We should be only about two hours from Bien Hoa, so will write more when I get there.

Love,

Wayne

CHAPTER FOUR

Arriving In-Country

My nerves were on edge as the plane approached the third world country where the United States had decided to go to war. It was daylight as the plane began its descent. I peered out the window and saw a lot of green landscape. Three quarters of the country consists of mountains and hills. It is approximately 8,712 miles from Hays, Kansas, to Ho Chi Minh City (formerly Saigon). When the aircraft landed at Bien Hoa Air Base, I was ready to disembark; it had been a long journey.

Bien Hoa Air Base

Bien Hoa Air Base is a former South Vietnamese Air Force and United States Air Force Base located in south-central southern Vietnam about twenty miles from Ho Chi Minh City near the city of Bien Hoa within Dong Nai Province. Stepping off the plane, I was tired and frightened, and the heat was stifling. The air was filled with smells of thousands of small charcoal stoves. It was a real culture shock seeing this small country for the first time. From Bien Hoa Air Base, we were transported to the 90th Replacement Battalion for in-country processing. Mesh wire covered the windows of the bus to protect us from Vietnamese children who might throw a grenade in the bus. It was sweaty and dusty as we journeyed through this unfamiliar territory.

April 4, 1967

Dear Mom and Dad,

Hi. We arrived here a few hours ago and boy is this place ever hurting. I got processed in and now waiting to be shipped out to my unit within 12 to 24 hours, but doubt it. I will send you my address when I get to my unit. It is something like 80 F here, but feels more like 110 F, as all I do is sweat. It rained a little this afternoon. We are only 25 miles out of Saigon, north. I hated this place the minute I stepped off the plane and more than likely will until I leave it. I would say that the average American would not believe what it is like over here. After seeing some of these people, I really feel sorry for them and the way they live. Well, I will write more later.

With love,

Wayne

"On the flight over here, we landed in Tokyo, Japan. They kept us on the plane until they could clear out the terminal. Then they let us off the plane while it was being serviced. Then it was back on the plane and on to Vietnam. After landing in Vietnam, we were put on a bus and sent to a troop replacement depot. During all of our training, we were told that the VC wore black pajamas. On the bus ride to the replacement depot, I noticed that everyone (all of the civilians) wore black pajamas. I thought, how do you tell the bad guys from the civilians?"
Ken Baldwin

April 6, 1967

Dear Mom and Dad,

Well, nothing new has happened for the last two days. I may be here for a week or two yet, but sure hope not, as we have hard labor details everyday. I'm starting to get adjusted to the heat now. I just took my first shower in over a week, so it really felt good, believe me. Oh yes, the only way you can get in contact with me is through the local Red Cross there. Well, I have some letters to write, so I will close for now. I'll write soon.

With love,

Wayne

April 7, 1967

Dear Mom and Dad,

Hi! Well, not much has happened in the last two days, except it seems like it is hotter! I had KP all night Wednesday, but got a pass to stay in the barracks and sleep some Thursday. It seems to stay cloudy most of the time here, but I have never seen a place so hot. I am still waiting to be shipped to my unit, but right now they do not seem to be shipping anyone to the 1st Cavalry, so I do not know how much longer I will be here. Boy, it sure seems like I am a long way from home. Time does not go very fast over here either. The days seem very long. Has it rained there very much lately? I hope everyone is fine there. I will close for now, as I cannot think of much more to say. I will write soon.

Love

Your Son,

Wayne

April 8, 1967

Dear Chuck,

How is the good care-free college life these days? Well, here I am, in the middle of No Man's Land. Right now, I am at the 90th Replacement Battalion, a few miles from Bien Hoa, 25 miles north of Saigon. I left Travis AFB last Sunday and from there to Seattle, WA International Airport, Tokyo, Japan International, Kadena

AFB Okinawa and finally Bien Hoa Air Base. While we are waiting around here to be shipped to our new units, they put us on details, such as burning human waste. There is not much fighting around here, they did kill four VCs a few hundred yards from here not too long ago, so I can hardly wait to leave this place, so I can see real action. I will be with the 1st Cavalry (airmobile) near An Khe. It is hotter than hell over here, believe me. Well, I had better close for now. I will send you my address as soon as I can. Tell Richer hi for me. Study hard and stay out of the Army.

Wayne

Spending my first twelve days in-country at the 90th Replacement Battalion was not much fun. I had a difficult time adjusting to the heat: I seemed to sweat all the time during the day, even in the shade. There was also fine red dirt that blew around the camp, making the place even more miserable.

We had to fall out in formation two or three times a day. The sergeant in charge of the newly arrived troops would call out names to assign us our duty for the day, or, hopefully, your name would be called out for shipment to your new unit. One of the worst duties you could be put on was to burn the previous day's feces. There were lines of outdoor toilets and each one contained a half of a fifty-five gallon barrel underneath the hole, which had to be removed and replaced with an empty barrel daily. The full barrel was then doused with jet fuel and lit to burn the excrement, causing a huge cloud of black smoke to rise into the air. There were other duties one could be put on, such as KP, carrying water, or barracks orderly detail.

One evening, coming out of the mess hall, I happened to meet a couple of officers on their way in for chow. Thinking we were in a war zone, it did not occur to me to salute them. Well, was I ever wrong! They stopped and reprimanded me for failing to recognize them. After leaving the replacement battalion for my new unit a few days later, saluting an officer was never again an issue.

Another evening I was at a club on base with some other guys I knew having a few beers. I was homesick and at the same time trying to adjust to my new environment. There was a jukebox in the bar and someone played "Detroit City" by Bobby Bare.

When he sang the chorus, "I want to go home/I want to go home/Oh, how I want to go home," I became very sad as I realized that if nothing bad happened, it would be a full year before I returned back to the World.

April 10, 1967

Bien Hoa,

South Vietnam

Dear Mom and Dad,

Well, today is the day because my name was finally called off for shipment. I know five other guys that are going with me. We leave by bus tonight from here and go to the Bien Hoa Air Base and from there fly to An Khe, 260 miles north of here. You can see where I will be on the map. An Khe is the home base of the 1st Air Cavalry Division. After we get there, we will be processed in and assigned to our new company by tomorrow night or Wednesday, and then receive five days of jungle training before going out in the field after Charlie. An Khe is located in the central highlands, 1,375 ft above sea level. I am going to be sending some money home soon, but I am going to keep most of my pay this time, so I can get a Polaroid camera that takes color pictures in 60 seconds. The 1st Cavalry home base is about 3 square miles in area and has five 10' high barbed wire fences about 100' apart around it with flood lights, so it would be rough for Charlie to get in there. I sure hope the weather is cooler up there, as I really hate this heat. It is about impossible to get any ice around here. Well, I will write more when I get my address in a few days and then you can have it put in the paper and my picture too, and give the paper my address, so they can send it to me. I guess that I had better quit for now and go turn my bedding in.

With love,

Wayne

April 11, 1967

Dear Mom and Dad,

Well, things did not work out the way it was planned, but maybe we were lucky things worked out the way they did. We left here last night at 10 p.m. for the Bien Hoa Air Base and our plane was supposed to leave for An Khe at 10:45 p.m., but the plane never made it down here to pick us up because some men were short of ammo and food, so they brought us back down here this morning and the earliest we can leave now is tomorrow. We ended up sleeping on a cement floor and eating C rations for breakfast. The VCs attacked the 1st Cavalry base at An Khe Saturday night with mortars, which killed nine and wounded quite a few. I sure hope they can get a plane to get us up to An Khe tomorrow. I will write more later.

Love,

Wayne

SAIGON (UPI) Communist troops Sunday, mortared the helicopter landing pad at An Khe, home of the 1st Air Cavalry Division in the central highlands and launched a fierce attack trying to overrun one of the main out-posts protecting the base.

While dozens of rounds of mortar shells pounded the landing pad,

Communist troops using small arms and hurling grenades swept toward the outpost manned by an Air Cavalry Fire team in the southwest part of the base.

The Americans turned back the attack with automatic weapons while armed helicopters with machine guns and rockets took off to search for the VC mortars.

The U.S. military command here said nine Americans were killed at the outpost and 15 others wounded. There were 8 Communists killed.

At the landing pad the mortar rounds damaged or destroyed five Chinook helicopters.

Two more Americans were wounded when one of the mortar rounds hit the Jeep they were driving.

The attack at An Khe was the first since September.

(Author's note: I cut this article out of a newspaper and mailed it home with my letter dated April 11, 1967)

April 13, 1967

Hi Mom and Dad,

I am still here at the 90th REPL BN, Bien Hoa and I am beginning to wonder if we are ever going to make it up to An Khe. Tomorrow will be my 10th day here, so it should not be long now. There sure was a lot of shooting going on around here last night, but I do not know why. It was enough to keep me awake for awhile though. I sure am getting tired of all this heat, but it does cool off some at night. The only thing I have done around here since last Monday is eat and sleep and keep off of hard labor details, which are not hard to get put on. Well, I hope everyone is fine back home.

With love

Your son,

Wayne

CHAPTER FIVE

Camp Radcliff

April 16, 1967

An Khe,

South Vietnam

Hi Folks,

I finally made it up here. I got to my new company last night. We got our jungle clothes and jungle boots and equipment this morning and rifle. I think starting tomorrow we will get three days of jungle training and then I will be out in the field on Operation Pershing. My company, "Charlie" is in the field now, but will be in by the 20th and then go back out in a few days. Helicopters fire machine guns around here all night to scare the VCs off. It is cooler up here, but will not start to rain until August. Well, I cannot think of much more to write for now. Please write soon. I will probably be in the field before I can get a letter, as it takes 10 days coming and going, five days each way.

With Love, Wayne

Standing next to a barracks at Camp Radcliff, the author is ready to go to the field.

April 16, 1967

An Khe

Hi Folks,

I already wrote you today, but they just gave me my weapon tonight, so I thought that I would write and tell you about it. I did not get an M-16 rifle, but an M-79 grenade launcher and an M-1911 45 caliber pistol. That is what I will carry unless something happens out in the field, so I might still carry an M-16 later on. I got me a new Vantage watch this afternoon at the PX that retails for $22.00. I got it for $16.50. I am going to wait until my R & R and then I am going to get a camera and tape recorder. Right now, things are pretty rough out in the field. I will write more later. Please write soon!

Your son,

Wayne

April 17, 1967

Dearest Mom, Dad and Brothers,

Hi! I have been on KP all day today. There seems to be a shortage of stationery, so I will not be able to write much longer until I get some, so I thought you could send me some and some air mail envelopes. You can send anything to me if it weighs less than 5 lbs at the regular postal rates airmail, so it should not cost very much. Not much has happened lately. I am still waiting to begin my three days of jungle training. I sure hope this week, as I hate KP! They sure feed us good here at base camp. We will get two hot meals out in the field every day and C rations once a day. My company is still out on Operation Pershing. Well, hope this finds everyone well. I am going to close for now, but I will write again soon. Write soon!

With love

Your son,

Wayne

1st Cavalry Training Center, Camp Radcliff, An Khe, South Vietnam.

April 21, 1967

1st Cavalry

Training Center

Dear Mom, Dad and Brothers,

Hi! I just finished my first day of training here, so I will be done with this training in three days. I will be out in the field by next Tuesday or Wednesday. The whole battalion came in from the field last Wednesday and go back out on the 24th. We will be near Bong Son in the An Lao Valley on Operation Pershing. I guess things are rough up there, as there are a lot of VCs. I got a camera yesterday. It is a Minolta-Matic 75. I gave $39 for it, but the processing is included in that, so I will send the film home to be developed and then it will be sent to you. I guess I can send film from the field. A few of them may not be any good because once the 10 second timer was set and I did not know it, so I thought I had taken a picture of a tent and once I forgot to take the lens cover off. They are color slides, so when you get them, you can write and tell me how they turned out. I also got a Sony radio, which is very nice. I am putting all of my money in an accrued account here, so when I come home, I will bring it all with me. I draw out $60 a month to spend. Please send some writing paper, as I cannot get any here. Well, it is about time for chow, so will close for now. Write soon!

With Love,

Wayne

The tower is forty feet up, but that doesn't stop these ambitious Cavalry men at the 1st Cavalry training center.
National Archives II file.

When I arrived at Camp Radcliff near An Khe, there were a number of specific details that needed to be completed before I was ready to go out in the field after "Charlie." Reporting to the supply room, I was issued jungle clothes, combat boots, field equipment, and a weapon. All new troops were required to attend in-country and First Cavalry Division orientation. Following the orientation, I went through three days of jungle training.

Part of the training was to learn how to rappel out of a Huey helicopter. At the training site, there was a forty-foot-high tower that the troops learned to rappel from. I hoped I would never have to use this training, but I realized it would be good to know in a real life-and-death situation.

There were normally four to six troops in each chopper for a combat air assault. In training, we were taught that one guy would be on each side of the slick (Huey), standing on the landing skid.

When we were ready to rappel, each one was to drop a good ten to fifteen feet down before stopping, because if you just jumped out, you took the risk of hitting the other guy or the bottom of the helicopter.

I spent ten days at Camp Radcliff preparing to go out in the field to fight the Viet Cong on Operation Pershing. I was very scared and did not know what to expect or what combat would be like. I could only hope and pray that my training had prepared me well. It was going to be a long year.

April 24, 1967

Dear Folks,

I finished my training and sure am glad , as it was rough. I was radioman and the radio got heavy. You would never believe how thick that jungle is. I am sending a picture, which is not very good, but you can see what my weapons look like. I carry about fifty rounds of ammo for that M-79 and it gets very heavy. I guess there are a lot of VCs up there. It really rains over here too, as last night I got completely soaked. Well, I am at the RCO club now and they are going to show a movie, so I will close for now. I will try to write more later. Please write.

Love,

Wayne

Ken Baldwin's account of his first month in-country

(Transcribed from taped interview)

"With our in-country training all completed, we were sent out to the field to join our new unit, which was the 3rd platoon, C Company 5th Battalion of the 7th Cavalry. After about three days out in the field, I, along with another guy (Marvin Dawkins), was assigned to an LRRP (Long Range Reconnaissance Patrol).

"They needed two new guys to join four experienced recon soldiers to go out on LLRP. They would clear out an area and insert us to do reconnaissance. We had to carry enough supplies to last a week.

"I can remember having some contact with the Viet Cong. One day, while on patrol, we found a spot to sit down and take a lunch break. They placed us out in the perimeter and I was setting up. There were rice paddy dikes in front of our position and a village on the far side of the dikes. We were kind of on a little hillock place, it had some hills and growing trees.

Marvin Dawkins poses with a Vietnamese boy, who is suspected of being a Viet Cong during Operation Pershing.

"I was sitting behind a low hedge, kind of leaning back to write a letter to another buddy of mine who was in the 1st Infantry in I Corps. All of a sudden, I heard somebody go Sh! Sh!.

"Everything got real still and you could hear people talking. They were walking around on that dike. There were six to eight VC. They were just walking alone, chatting away. I remember one guy had on a baseball cap, but I cannot remember which team. There were a couple of women with them. I could almost reach out and touch them. They were only four or five feet away from us.

"Fortunately for us, they didn't even realize our presence in the area. We were all lying right out in the open. They walked right by us and crossed the rice paddy dikes and on into the village. We then called for artillery strikes on the village. We were sitting watching all of this, when all of a sudden, I see the guy with the baseball cap come running out of the village. I told that to the patrol leader and he said, 'Okay, we are out of here.' We all saddled up and went to the top of the hill on the other side and called to be picked up and pulled out of there. That

28

was a scary one.

"You were out there all by yourselves, there were just the six of us. You were just to go out there and see what kind of movements the enemy was making and report back. We were supposed to see and not be seen. The last couple of weeks that I was involved with the LRRPs, they wanted us to set up night ambushes. When there were just six of us out in the boonies, carrying everything on your back that you needed for a week, you were kind of limited as to what you could take with you. Fortunately, I got off that detail."

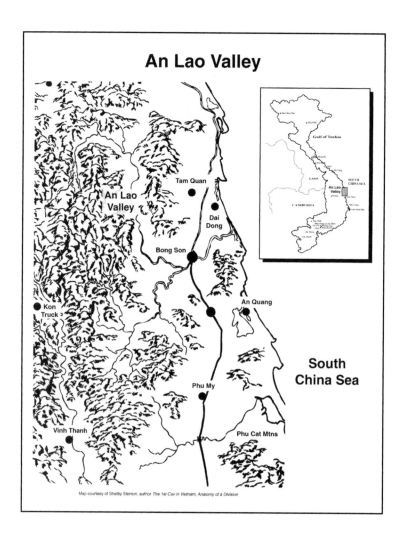

Map courtesy of Shelby Stanton, author *The 1st Cav in Vietnam, Anatomy of a Division*

CHAPTER SIX

Operation Pershing

In February 1967, Operation Pershing began in a territory that was familiar to many sky troopers (a sky trooper is a 1st Cavalry Division combat infantryman who rides a helicopter into battle): the Bong Son Plains in northern Binh Dinh Province. For the first time, the 1st Cavalry Division committed all three of its brigades in the same area.

ARVN soldiers familiar with methods of the Viet Cong in the Bong Son Plain helped the sky troopers locate and eliminate the numerous caves and tunnels infiltrated by the enemy. For nearly a year, the division scoured the Bong Son Plains, An Lao Valley, and the hills of costal II Corps, seeking out the enemy units and their sanctuaries. Pershing became a tedious, unglamorous mission that produced eighteen major engagements and numerous minor skirmishes in the eleven-month campaign.

The division began 1968 by terminating Operation Pershing, the longest of the 1st Cavalry's Vietnam actions. When the operation ended on 21 January, the enemy had lost 5,410 soldiers and 2,400 enemy soldiers had been captured. In addition, some 1,300 individual and 137 crew weapons had been captured or destroyed.[3]

April 26, 1967

Dear Mom and Dad,

   Well, this is to let you know I am out in the field now in the An Lao Valley. Not much has happened so far. <u>*We overran a VC village this afternoon and got a VC girl and boy.*</u> *A piece of shrapnel landed a few feet from me this morning also. I sent a roll of film to be developed, so you should have them sometime next month. Well, I had better close for now and get ready for the night. Please write.*

With love

Your son,

Wayne

5th Battalion 7th Cavalry Staff Journals or Officer's Log

26 Apr 67

1215 hr C Co to TOC: in checking out bunkers we have found no caves or tunnels. Have found approx 100 ears of corn in one bunker, are destroying. Have detained 4 persons, **One is a girl, 16 years old. The guide says that she is definitely VC. One is a boy, 16 yrs old; guide says he is not a VC**. Other 2 are small children.

1220 hr C Co to TOC: have linked up with the tank platoon, are moving out at this time.

1252 hr C Co to TOC: reference bombings; made a lot of craters, but did no apparent damage to the bunker complexes.

1341 hr C Co to TOC: have reached the southern end of the village and have linked up with C Co 1/7 Cav.

1425 hr C Co to TOC: have checked out individuals along river. are mostly women and children.

2020 hr C Co to TOC: at approximately 2025 Hr OP to east outside of CP, observed what appeared to be several individuals, silhouetted, OP engaged with small arms fire, the fire was returned, negative assessment at this time.

2033 hr C Co to TOC: LP is observing quite a bit of movement in village that they swept through today, movement generally to NE.

2120 hr C Co to TOC: LP 1 says that the movement has terminated, since they brought in artillery, however C Co says that they are going to work the village over with heavy artillery.

2135 hr C Co to TOC: LP 1 reports negative signs of further movement will continue to bring artillery in on it.

2145 hr *T*o TOC from all units: SITREP Green

SUMMARY

C Co maneuvered its force in conjunction with B Co and Tank Platoon, swept south into suspected enemy village with negative enemy contact. **1215 hrs 4 detainees were apprehended in village, 3 were later released.** 1341 hrs element completed its sweep through village and joined C Co 1/7 Cav, and closed BS 737043 with 3 ambush patrols. 2025 hrs enemy with small arms fire engaged after perimeter OP observed several enemy in village vic BS 747053. Arty concentration called with negative results.

April 29, 1967

An Lao Valley

Hi Chuck,

How are things with you these days? What are your plans for this summer? Boy, this is a real SOB over here! I have been in the field for five days now and will not get to go back in until late June, so that makes it a long time to stay out here with the

VCs. Today, we got airlifted by helicopter to this village and we went through it and burned and killed everything. I killed a pig with my .45 pistol. Well, I had better close for now as we are getting ready to move out. Please write soon.

Your Brother,

Wayne

Cavalry men drive the local Vietnamese people south from their homes toward refugee camps.

29 Apr 67

0415 hr C Co to TOC: Patrol 2 heard some noises to the W and slightly S of their location. They are going to fire some artillery in that area.

0458 hr C Co to TOC: Artillery has finished firing in the area where patrol heard movement. No assessment at this time, movement has stopped.

0657 hr C Co to TOC: C Co says he will recon the area where arty just fired at BS 754016 at 0700 hrs.

1045 hr C Co to TOC: 1st lift off at 1045 hrs from BS 760015 to BS 745086.

1206 hr C Co to TOC: SPOT REPORT – At 1205 hrs at BS 743083 found 1 crock containing 100 lbs of rice, and 1 57mm RR casing; it appears to be about 1 month old.

1324 hr C Co to TOC: SPOT REPORT – At 1310 hrs at BS 751129 my 16 element found a sleeping area for approx 20 individuals, also found 110 lbs of rice and numerous trails freshly used going west to the high ground. Also found 3 clips of M-1 ammo freshly oiled, a rice machine and 1 US helmet liner. Destroyed rice and machine.

1738 hr C Co to TOC: Hear automatic weapons fire approx 300 meters to N, 36 elements at BS 739061 is the one who hears the firing.

1918 hr C Co to TOC: Final locations – (-) at BS 747055, patrol 1 at BS 749029, patrol 2 at BS 736054, and patrol 3 at BS 739071.

2050 hr SITREP Green All units each hour.

SUMMARY

C Co was in a stand still posture until 1100 hrs and C Co combat assaulted at 1045 hrs into LZ at BS 745085 with TD at 1113 hrs. They swept south and closed at BS747055. Two platoons (1st & 4th) moved on foot north on night patrol and ambush mission on the An Lao Valley floor from previous night's CP location.

Troops skinny-dipping in a river. It was about the only way a guy could clean up once in a while. Photo courtesy of Ken Baldwin

May 1, 1967

An Lao Valley

Dearest Mom, Dad and Brothers,

I was sure glad to receive your letter today. This was the first time I received mail ever since I got here, as I got six letters today. We took a bath in a river yesterday and I got a little sunburn, so it really makes it rough carrying that pack around now. Yesterday evening, we were going out on an ambush when we spotted six VC and killed five of them near a village, but could not get down there until this morning and they had dragged all the bodies away. They also called an air strike in on that village last night and that was really something to see as they really tore the place up. Tomorrow we are being airlifted way up north to some mountains, which is really going to be rough, as there are a lot of mines, traps and Charlie's (VC) up there. It is not near as bad as I thought it would be, but I have not been in a big fire fight yet, so I do not know. About all we do is chase after the VCs. They are always running, but when they do stop and fight, you sure know about it. I keep cutting my arms and hands up from all the bushes and it takes forever to heal. My feet bother me some too. Well, I had better close for now. I hope this finds everyone well and doing fine!

With Love,

PFC Wayne

B-52 conducting an air strike.

My First Weeks in the Field

In my entire life, I had never ridden on a helicopter until one day, loaded down with all my gear and weapons, I climbed onto a Huey and flew out to the field to join my company. The chopper made a deafening roar as we lifted off. My fellow newbies on board and I were headed into uncharted territory. My mind was racing ahead with uncertain thoughts. What would it be like to face the enemy for the first time? How would I react in my first combat situation? The seat of my consciousness was filled with questions, mostly my fear of the unknown. The reality was, I was an FNG (fucking new guy) and had a lot to learn from the older, more experienced grunts in my company.

Jumping off the chopper for the first time, I hit the ground running as the blades from the helicopter made a whap-wop-wop-wop-whap sound above my head. The company was camped on the Bong Son Plains. Looking to the west, one could see the rugged An Lao mountain ranges. To the east over the horizon was the South China Sea. The area where we were camped was shaded by palm trees. The countryside was a vivid, lush scene of greenery.

I made my way around the camp and was introduced to several of the guys in my platoon. Many of them were short-timers, as they had been in-country for almost a year and were about to be rotated back to the States. I envied them. They had spent their time in Nam and now it was my turn. It wouldn't be long until I started to count the days until I also could return home.

That night, I pulled my first guard duty. I was scared and apprehensive; however, my shift quietly went by with no sign of the enemy. The nights in Vietnam can be very dark and scary. I remember one night when I was sent out to man an LP (listening post). The LP was about 100 yards out in front of our perimeter of defense. The LP served as a first warning in case the enemy was detected and about to attack our camp. Every noise made me frightened that "Victor Charlie" (the Viet Cong) was sneaking up on my position, intent on killing me before I could warn the company of the impending assault.

During my first weeks in the field, I received my combat initiation when we killed five Viet Cong near a village. We also burned villages to the ground, killed livestock, and destroyed the Vietnamese food supply. In the process, I was becoming more hardened to the realities of war. I was beginning to realize that war is grim. It was not the way it had been traditionally portrayed in the movies and on television, where it often seemed glamorous, maybe even fun.

My mind and body were undergoing a change from the daily grind of going on combat patrols, sometimes on trails in the dense jungle, other times through flooded rice paddy fields. I became sunburned, my arms and hands were cut by the bushes, and I suffered from immersion-foot (jungle rot). After a few weeks in the field, my exposure to the rigors of combat had toughened me up, both physically and mentally.

The Old Man in the Village

One night our company was camped in the An Lao Mountains overlooking the valley below our position. During the night while I was on guard duty, I watched in awe as a B-52 carpet bombed a village down in the valley. It was a spectacular show of American firepower.

"After a decade of preparing for strategic bombing campaigns with nuclear weapons, the B-52 finally first went to war in 1965 in Vietnam, as part of Operation Arc Light. This campaign carried out tactical carpet-bombing of South Vietnam, an assignment for which the plane was not equipped and the crews were not trained; consequently, the results were not good."[4]

This once picturesque ancestral village was now reduced to rubble. The following morning our platoon conducted a sweeping operation through the village, looking for any sign of life.

"Therefore, this area was mostly all free-fire zones. So it was this understanding that it was a free-fire zone that everything was fair game. If at any time, you saw people in any way trying to avoid you, run away, or make suspicious movements, they were free game. You could go ahead, shoot, and kill them."[5]

As the platoon patrolled toward the southern edge of the village, we passed by a hedgerow. At the time of this incident, I was the radioman for the platoon. As we continued working our way south, I happened to glance over my left shoulder where I spotted an old Vietnamese man rising up in plain sight. I asked the lieutenant what we should do. He gave the order to kill him.

I have vivid memories of watching as the platoon opened fire with their M-16s and the old man slowly fell to the ground, mortally wounded. That scene is forever frozen in my conscience. In my mind, killing an innocent old man was hard to justify, even though we were in a free-fire zone and the body count was used to show that the United States was winning the war.

Years of watching movies where the Nazis mowed down innocent civilians stimulated moral outrage, and now we were doing the same thing. Free-fire zones or the need for body counts were not sufficient to override my sense of guilt for such actions.

During the Vietnam War, enemy body counts became a regular feature in military statements intended to demonstrate progress. But the statistics ended up proving poor indicators of the war's course. Pressure on U.S. units to produce high death tolls led to inflated tallies, which significantly impaired the Pentagon's credibility.

"In Vietnam, we were pursuing a strategy of attrition, so body counts became the measure of performance for military units," said Conrad C. Crane, director of the military history institute at the U.S. Army War College. "But the numbers got so wrapped up with career aspirations that they were sometimes falsified."[6]

Body Count

Body count refers to the total number of people killed in a particular event. In combat, the body count is often based on the number of confirmed kills, but occasionally only an estimate. The military gathers such figures for a variety of reasons, such as determining the need for continuing operations, estimating efficiency of new and old weapons, and planning follow-up operations.

Ho Chi Minh

Vietnam War

Since the goal of the United States in the Vietnam War was not to conquer North Vietnam, but rather to ensure the survival of the South Vietnamese government, measuring progress was difficult. All the contested territory was theoretically "held" already. Instead, the U.S. Army used body counts to show that the United States was winning the war. The Army's theory was that eventually, the Viet Cong and North Vietnamese Army would lose due to attrition.

It was rumored that Ho Chi Minh once said, in reference to the French, "You can kill ten of our men for every one we kill of yours. But even at those odds, you will lose and we will win." Most analysis of war casualties indicates that the allied army inflicted roughly a three-to-two ratio of communist combat deaths against allied deaths.[7] Ho Chi Minh was proved correct in that the United States eventually pulled out.

May 2, 1967

Hi again. We were supposed to have made an air assault this morning way up north of here on a mountain, but last night the 2nd platoon got hit by VC while they were on ambush. A lieutenant got hit by a machine gun. I am in the 3rd platoon, 1st squad. I also went on an ambush last night, but did not see much action. Please write soon. We have been in the field for eight days now and do not expect to go back in until June or July.

Your son,

Wayne

1 May 67

0643 hr C Co to TOC: time 0630, at BS 763035 16 element picked up one female, approx 25 yrs old, she was coming out of the village where C Co had their contact last night. She had blood stains on her, was wearing blue shirt and black bottoms, and also had 3 or 4 shirts with her. Our interpreter is going to talk to her, keep advised.

0658 hr C Co to TOC: time 0655H at BS 762045 found one crock of rice hidden in the underbrush. Crock contained approx 150 lbs of rice, will destroy.

0718 hr C Co to TOC: time 0715 at BS 760039 found 3 small sacks of rice, 1 pair of black PJ's, one pair of sandals. Negative bodies as of yet.

0740 hr C Co to TOC: time 0740, at BS 763036 found a combination of clothing, all of these clothes were new and well tailored, and colors were black, blue, gray, and brown. Total of 6-8 complete suits, all were destroyed.

0743 hr C Co to TOC: time 0730 at BS 764034 found 120 lbs of rice, was destroyed, was found in a crock hidden in the bushes.

1046 hr C Co to TOC: time 1040 at BS 768008 found 300 lbs of rice, 2 lbs of salt in a well camouflaged crock, all was destroyed.

1924 hr C Co to TOC: request MED EVAC for one man with 104.6 temperature, at BS 755043, LZ is secure, standing by with illumination.

1943 hr C Co to TOC: MED EVAC for one man is completed at this time.

1944 hr C Co to TOC: change in location for patrol 1, now at BS 752028.

2012 hr C Co to TOC: time 2010 patrol 1 just had a trip flare tripped, reacted by setting off of a claymore mine, will keep us advised.

2012 hr C Co to TOC: location of the trip flare incident is BS 751028.

2042 hr C Co to TOC: <u>**reference patrol 1 contact receiving small arms fire from 3 automatic weapons, have 1 friendly WIA**</u>, now requesting MED EVAC artillery being called in at this time.

2143 hr C Co to TOC: MED EVAC for C Co complete at this time.

SUMMARY

C Co continued mission on the valley floor with one light enemy contact. At 0630 hrs vic BS 76035 the 1st platoon apprehended one female detainee. At approx 1600 hrs the 1st platoon closed LZ Laramie for security mission for Bn fire base and arty positions. At 2010 hr vic BS 751028 ambush patrol 32 engaged 3 VC with weapons when VC tripped a flare. Claymore mine was immediately set off and ambush opened fire, with no return from enemy. Estimate 3 VC KIA. <u>**Platoon leader and one man investigated area under cover of the patrol, when they came under AW fire from unknown size enemy force, resulting in 1 US WIA.**</u> Patrol 1 countered with small arms fire and managed to extract the individuals, and immediate artillery and mortar fire saturated the area. No further assessment of enemy casualties.

May 5, 1967

An Lao Valley

Dear Mom, Dad and Brothers,

I will write you a few lines this afternoon. I am sending a picture of Company C, 5th Battalion, 7th Cavalry on an air assault. I have been on one so far and like riding in the helicopter, but I do not like jumping off as it means a lot of walking. Lately, I have been carrying a claymore mine and mortar rounds with me plus my pack and ammo, so it really gets heavy. <u>I do not know if you want to hear something like this or not, but anyway, today we were searching a village and found some fresh graves and nobody else would uncover it, so I did and found three dead VC.</u> So far, the food has been real good except for the C rations, as they usually bring two hot *meals out here a day. My mail seems to come all at once or not at all. One day, I got six letters, none the next one, the next eight and none yesterday, so do not know what I will get today. How does the wheat look this year? I am doing fine except the heat is hard to take. Write.*

Love

Your son,

Wayne

5 May 67

0921 hr C Co to TOC: At 0915 at BR 760997 my 15 element came across 50 rds of AK-47 ammo in a bunker found a rucksack with

M-18 Claymore mine

notebook also. Est. 1 VC WIA because of blood trail. We destroyed the bunker. At 0910 hrs at BS 761998 36 element found approx 1200 lbs of rice in crocks, bags, cans. Being destroyed.

1215 hr C Co to TOC: We have picked up one man in vic of contact last night (BS754984), individual says he was a rice carrier for the VC and he pointed out some locations where he took rice for pick up. He was wearing khaki shirt and light shorts, will be tagged as VCS also. Location BS 754984.

1413 hr <u>C Co to TOC: at BS 761997 found 3 fresh graves, dug them up, found 3 VC KIA wrapped in poncho type material.</u>

1420 hr C Co to S3 Air: at BR 762998 35 element picked up one VCS trying to evade to the southeast into the hills, was dressed in black and about 35 yrs of age.

SUMMARY

C Co continued search and destroy mission sweeping south with one element working generally around Check Point Willie (BR 785955), denying refugees and villagers entry into the An Lao Valley. 1110H, 2nd platoon was relieved of security mission in place by 2nd platoon, D Co and returned to C Co (touch down 1121H) control. 1215H, 1 VCS (claiming to be a rice carrier) was apprehended. 1405H, vic BS 759989, **3 VC KIA (BC) were found in a freshly dug grave as a result of ARA wounds from previous night (1855H), sighting and ARA strike, dressed in black PJ's, wrapped in poncho type material.** 1420H, vic BR 762998, 3rd platoon (patrol 35) apprehended one VCS trying to evade. 1825H, vic BR 760985 2nd platoon (patrol 2A), spotted 10 enemy, 2 with weapons. Scout ship assisted ground element, enemy moved into a village at 1859 hrs and were engaged with mortars and ARA ships with negative assessment. C Co closed BR 766988 with 3 ambush patrols.

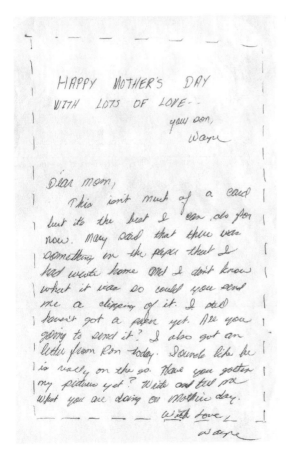

HAPPY MOTHER'S DAY
WITH LOTS OF LOVE--
your son,
Wayne

Dear mom,
This isn't much of a card but it's the best I can do for now. Mary said that there was something in the paper that I had wrote home and I don't know what it was so could you send me a clipping of it. I still haven't got a paper yet. Are you going to send it? I also got an letter from Ron today. Sounds like he is really on the go. Have you gotten my pictures yet? Write and tell me what you are doing on mothers day.
With love,
Wayne

Western Kansas World

April 27, 1967
Men In Service
Arrives in Vietnam

Wayne Purinton writes that he arrived in Bien Hoa, South Vietnam April 4 by way of San Francisco, Seattle, Tokyo and Okinawa. The weather seems much hotter than the 80 degrees it registers.

"April 16, 1967 – I arrived at An Khe Air Base, where I will meet my company, Charlie. They are on Operation Pershing, but will be in about the 20th and then go back out in a few days. I will carry an M-79 grenade launcher and an M-1911 45 caliber pistol.

"Helicopters fire machine guns around here all night to keep the VCs off. It is cooler up here and will not start to rain until August. They feed us good here at base camp. We will get two hot meals out in the field every day and C rations once a day."

He would like to hear from his friends: PFC Leonard Wayne Purinton, U.S. 55984209, Co C, 5th Battalion, 7th Cavalry, 1st Air Cavalry (Airmobile), A P O San Francisco, Calif. 96490.

May 8, 1967
LZ Sandra

Dear Mom, Dad and Brothers,

I got your letter this morning and am real glad to hear from you. We were airlifted yesterday morning from the An Lao Valley up here to LZ Sandra, which is on top of a mountain to secure it and hope to be here until the 12th and then probably go back down in the valley. I can see the Red China Sea from here, so will get some pictures of it, and are only about 15 miles from the DMZ, so we are way up here in the corner of South Vietnam. I have not had a hair cut since I left California, so guess I will have to get one this morning. I traded my M-79 and pistol to another guy for an M-16 rifle yesterday, which makes my pack lighter and I like the 16 better. I am going to try and zero it in this afternoon. Who won the league track meet this year? How did the prom turn out? It is a lot cooler up here on the mountain as I got cold last night. How is the irrigation coming so far? I cannot think of much more for now, so will close. Please write soon.

With love
Your son,
Wayne

May 9, 1967

Dear Mom, Dad and Brothers,

I received a letter and writing paper this evening and sure glad to get it. I also got a letter from Aunt Becky today. I forgot to tell you to send me some things that I need, so maybe you can send them soon. A toothbrush, pens and some cookies or something. There really is not much new with me. We are supposed to be here until the 12th or maybe longer and we are on a 30 minute standby in case some company gets hit, so that means we could be dropped right into the middle of a fire fight. Who won the league track meet this year? Well, I cannot think of much more for now, so will close. I am sure glad to receive your letters, so write.

With love, Wayne

C Company, 5th Battalion, 7th Cavalry making a combat air assault during Operation Pershing. Photo courtesy of Ken Baldwin

May 13, 1967

An Lao Mountains

Dear Mom and Dad,

Well, this is the first chance I have had to write since Wednesday, as we left LZ Sandra and have been in the mountains for the last three days. These mountains are really rough. Sometimes, the underbrush gets so thick we have to cut our way through and it might take one hour to go 100 yards. I really got my arms and hands cut up from the thorn trees and grass, which gets up to 16 feet high. We should make it to the bottom of the valley by tonight and then I heard we are making an air assault tomorrow up north near the DMZ. <u>Yesterday, the 1ˢᵗ platoon killed 16 VC and only had 2 WIAs, so that was not too bad.</u> What is new back home? How is the irrigation coming along? Are you not going to send me the World? I sure would like to get it as we do not get many papers to read. When does Ronnie graduate?

Well, I cannot think of much more to write, so will close for now. Please write.

With love,

Wayne

During the Vietnam War, the troops were constantly moved from one area to the next. It was easy for the soldier to become confused about where his unit was located. Such confusion was due to a lack of understanding about Vietnam's geography and the rumor mill of the unit. According to my letter dated May 8, 1967, I thought we were near the DMZ. In my letter dated May 13, 1967, I thought we were going to make an air assault up north near the Demilitarized Zone, but in reality, our area of operation was approximately 220 miles south of the DMZ.

12 May 67

1030 hr C Co to TOC: at BS 760193 16 & 26 elements spotted 3 VC to their front, 2 males and 1 female, 1 VC KIA with web gear, poncho, pistol belt.

1032 hr C Co to TOC: 16 element now in pursuit with 26 element on the left acting as a blocking force.

1038 hr C Co to TOC: VC KIA was the female, wearing black PJ's, NVA type camouflage hat, pistol belt, poncho, web gear, no weapon, at BS 777186.

1059 hr C Co to TOC: 16 & 26 at BS 757196 have VC movement to their rear, request gunships; contact was made again in the thick brush.

1110 hr C Co to TOC: addition to spot report about one VC KIA (female), also was carrying a ruck sack with medical supplies and food.

1112 hr C Co to TOC: one more VC KIA with khaki uniform with one hand grenade (Chicom type) also at another location found 6 hammocks, 7 ruck sacks, 4 pistol belts, and one blood trail heading southwest, more to follow (vic BS 777186)

1220 hr C Co to TOC: **time 1210H at BS 755188 1st platoon killed 3 VC,** dressed in green khaki uniforms, individuals were hiding in a natural cave, 4 ft high and 10 ft deep, 1st platoon found one Chicom grenade 200 rounds of AK-47 ammo now checking out the cave for hidden weapons.

1250 hr C Co to TOC: time 1245 reference **3 VC KIA in the natural cave BS 755188 1st platoon** found one entrenching tool, 4 gas masks, with clear plastic, numerous items of women clothing, numerous bandages, one of the VC had an old wound which was healing, appeared that this cave might have been used as some type of aid station, at the rear of the cave there is a small hole leading back into the mountain, also found some documents in the cave, some of the documents were dated as late as May 1, 1967.

1300 hr C Co to TOC: 1st platoon spotted one individual who fled 1st platoon now in pursuit, 2d platoon in blocking position.

1430 hr C Co to TOC: time 1430 **1st platoon at BS 755187 ran across 2 VC, 2 VC tried to evade, results 2 VC KIA** (BC), were wearing khaki uniforms, both VC had 2 US type grenades, they are 19-25 yrs old.

1431 hr C Co to TOC: **1st platoon time 1431 at BS 756188 killed one VC** dressed in green clothing individual had one US hand grenade, and he tried to evade. Time 1440 location BS 766188 2nd platoon came across another VC dressed in light green uniform, VC had a grenade, wooden handle type, tried to flee results 1 VC KIA (BC).

1505 hr C Co to TOC: 1st platoon had 4-6 VC pinned in a cave at BS 766188.

1535 hr C Co to TOC: time 1530 at BS 755186 **1st platoon found and took under fire, 6 VC, results, 6 VC KIA** (BC), 4 dressed in black.

1608 hr C Co to TOC: time 1600 at BS 755185 **1st platoon found in a cave 1 VC KIA body** dressed in black PJ's, was 19-20 yrs old, body was there about 2-3 days. Also found 2 ruck sacks containing rice and change of clothing, also 2 more ruck sacks containing medical supplies, found one grave unoccupied on the outside of cave.

1627 hr C Co to TOC: request MED EVAC **for one man wounded by a sniper with an AK-47,** at BS 75183, wounded in the leg.

1636 hr C Co to TOC: request my 1st & 2nd platoons stay where they are at this time, at BS 754183, they are still receiving sniper fire at this location. They have spotted approx 6 VC in this location, are still checking this area.

1652 hr C Co to TOC: time 1706 at BS 726220 1st 6 sorties of A Co lifted off to LZ BS 804216.

1720 hr C Co to TOC: time 1720 1st 6 sorties of A Co put down on the LZ at BS 804216 at this time, LZ secure, negative contact.

MED EVAC Helicopter

1722 hr C Co to TOC: <u>**have one WIA at the same location individual was hit in the hip,**</u> will need a hoist to get them out, MED EVAC notified.

1905 hr C Co to TOC: one individual MED EVAC at this time.

1915 hr C Co to TOC: <u>**at this time have two WIA.**</u>

1920 hr C Co to TOC: MED EVAC completed at this time.

2050 hr To TOC from all units: SITREP Green

SUMMARY

C Co continued its search and destroy, southwest from previous day (BS 780196) location. Element broken into 2 separate maneuver elements working on the west and east along the trail route. 1030H, vic BS 760193, 1st and 2nd platoons spotted 3 VC (one female) along trail route, 1st platoon pursued with 2nd platoon on its left as blocking force, engaged enemy (BS 757193) resulting in 1 VC KIA (female). 1112H, same general locale, 1 VC KIA hiding in thick brush. 1220H, vic BS 755188, 1st platoon engaged 3 VC hiding in cave, results 3 VC KIA (BC). 1430H, vic BS 755187, 1st platoon engaged 2 VC trying to evade, results 2 VC KIA (BC). 1440H, vic BS 756188, 2nd platoon engaged 1 VC trying to evade, result 1 VC KIA (BC).

May 16, 1967

An Lao Valley

Dearest Mom and Dad,

I will write a few lines now as I am on an ambush patrol and am waiting for it to get dark. We have been in the mountains for the last seven days, so have not gotten much mail or hot chow lately. Just C rations and water. We got back down in the valley and joined the rest of the company this afternoon. <u>One of the guys in my platoon, the point man, was killed by a sniper two days ago and we killed one VC, while up in the mountains.</u> This afternoon, we found a herd of water buffalo by the river and they told us to shoot them. I got my first hot chow in days this afternoon and of all things it had to rain. I heard that we are going in from the field June 13th. I sure hope so, as I have been in the field for a month now, but time goes fast out here. I am thinking about extending my tour to six more months over here and be a machine gunner in a helicopter. That way, I could get out of the field and infantry and would also get a new MOS (Military Occupational Specialty). It would mean $100 flight pay more a month after nine months, a free trip home and back for a month and two R & R's. It would be a lot safer than being out here in the field. Well, cannot think of much more to write, so will close. I hope everyone is well. Write!

With love

Your son,

Wayne

P.S. If we stay down in the valley I will be able to write more often.

14 May 67

0845 hr C Co to TOC: 1ˢᵗ lift off the ground at this time enroute to LZ EAGLE (BS 775166).

0908 hr C Co to TOC: 2d and final lift touch down at LZ EAGLE at this time, lift now complete with negative enemy contact on the LZ.

0921 hr C Co to TOC: 1ˢᵗ lift into LZ RIDGE (BS 773197) at this time, negative contact, LZ secure.

1045 hr C Co to TOC: locations:1ˢᵗ, 4ᵗʰ platoons and CP at BS 777166, 2d & 3d platoons at BS 764194.

1154 hr C Co to TOC: at BS 763195 1ˢᵗ platoon found one more VC KIA where they had the action on the 12ᵗʰ of May, KIA was killed by artillery body was dressed in black PJ's.

1651 hr C Co to TOC: 2d & 3d plts have made contact with unknown size enemy force at BS 758194. Receiving heavy automatic weapons fire coming from due west. At this time we have one US KIA.

1707 hr C Co to TOC: Co XO says he thinks there are 2 AW and 2-3 SA out there. Believes VC is moving W. 3d plt maneuvering to cut them off.

1711 hr C Co to S3: 3d Plt has both of his flanks marked. ARA is ready to go in.

1716 hr C Co to TOC: **We have 1 KIA, this individual was point man – alerted other members of the patrol of the ambush before he was KIA.**

1719 hr C Co to TOC: have broken contact at this time; believe VC is fleeing to the west. Are going to put artillery into the area at this time.

1743 hr C Co to TOC: my 3d platoon action was not an ambush as previously reported this was a sniper action; believe it was 2 snipers with automatic weapons.

1935 hrs C Co to TOC: time 1935 at BS 757194 26 & 36 position is being probed at this time. One of the booby traps was tripped, think they got one VC.

2150 hr To TOC from all units: SITREP Green

SUMMARY

C Co conducted 2 separate combat assaults. 2d & 3d plts combat assaulted at 0845 hrs into LZ RIDGE, BS 773197 with TD at 0900 hrs. C Co combat assaulted at 0908 hrs into LZ EAGLE, BS 775166, with TD at 0931 hrs. At 1154 hrs vic BS 763195

2d plt discovered 1 VC KIA by arty from 12 May action. At 1651 hrs vic BS758194 the 2d & 3d Plts came in contact with unknown size enemy force believed to be 2 VC with AW. **Initial fire was heavy, cutting off the point man who warned the others of the sniper ambush which resulted in 1 US KIA.** 3d Plt maneuvered in force to cut off the enemy trying to flee W. ARA was on station with scout ships assisting ground forces. Contact was broken at 1719 hrs and arty called in. Upon lifting of arty scout ships recon'd by fire in the area with negative assessment. C Co closed at BS 775165 and 2d & 3d Plts closed at BS 767194. At 1935 hrs vic BS 757194 2d & 3d Plts perimeter was probed by unknown size enemy force who tripped a booby trap, estimate 1 VC KIA.

A member of D Co 1/7 Cavalry 1ˢᵗ Air Cavalry Division reads the New Testament on a short break on a sweep of the An Lao Valley. The rifleman, rifle in hand, the Bible in the other, sits on an ammo box ready for action. National Archives II file

CHAPTER SEVEN

The Things I Carried

The things I carried were partly a function of rank, partly of field specialty. During my one-year tour of duty, I held a variety of positions. I arrived out in the field as a green Private First Class (E-3) carrying an M-79 grenade launcher, which weighed 5.9 pounds unloaded, a reasonably light weapon except for the ammunition, which was heavy. A single round weighed ten ounces. I would typically carry forty or more rounds. I also carried an M-1911 .45 caliber pistol. I was not very happy carrying these weapons, as I felt they offered very little protection in a firefight.

After a few weeks in the field, I was able to trade weapons with another guy in the platoon and started carrying the M-16. The guy I traded weapons with was later killed in action. The standard M-16 gas-operated assault rifle weighed 7.5 pounds unloaded, 8.2 pounds with its full 20-round magazine. Depending on numerous factors, such as the topography and psychology, the rifleman carried anywhere from twelve to twenty magazines, usually in cloth bandoliers, adding on another 8.4 pounds at minimum, 14 pounds maximum. When it was available, I also carried M-16 maintenance gear, which included a rod, steel brush, swabs, and tubes of LSA oil. These items weighed a pound.

About one month into my tour, I became the RTO (radio telephone operator) for my squad. The PRC-25 radio weighed twenty-six pounds with its battery. A few weeks later, I became the head RTO for the 3rd platoon, which meant I followed the lieutenant around while we were on patrol. Carrying the radio had its perks. Mainly I knew what was happening at the company level, but it was a real burden to carry out in the jungle and rice paddies. The life expectancy of a radio operator in a firefight was about fifteen seconds. With that big antenna sticking in the air, it was like saying: "Here I am, shoot me!"

Author on patrol carrying the PRC-25 radio, which weighted twenty-six pounds.

I carried the radio for about three months before going back to the rear and being hospitalized for an infection in my leg. When I returned to the field a week later, I went back to carrying the M-16 rifle and M-60 machine gun ammo for Lee Danielson's 4th squad. I usually carried between ten to fifteen pounds of M-60 ammunition draped in belts across my chest and shoulders.

The things I carried were largely determined by necessity. Among those necessities were a P-38 can opener, pocket knife, heat tabs for C-rations, wristwatch, dog tags, mosquito repellent, chewing gum, candy, cigarettes, salt tablets, lighter, matches, writing tablet, envelopes, pen, poncho, C-rations, and two or three canteens of water. Together, these items weighed between fifteen and twenty pounds.

May 17, 1967

Dear Mom, Dad and Brothers,

Hi! I will write a few lines to let you know that everything is ok with me. I have a new job now. I am RTO (radioman) for my squad. That is 26 lbs more, so I have a big load to carry now (50 lbs), but think I will make it ok. You said you got the picture. How is the color, light or dark or anything like that? I sure like my new camera, but it is too big to carry out here in the field, so may get a 104 later on. If you can get some prints from them, please do, as would like to see them. I am still debating whether to extend six more months and be a machine gunner and probably will not decide until next month as the whole battalion may go into An Khe. I am going on ambush patrol tonight. I received a letter from a girl in Damar today. She sent her picture and is very nice-looking. She is 18. Well, we are getting ready to move out on ambush, so better close. Will try to write more later.

With love,

Wayne

May 21, 1967

Dear Mom and Dad,

Will write a few lines now as this is the first spare time I have had in quite a while. Two days ago, A company was surrounded by VC, so we were airlifted in there to help them out. They had a big fire fight, 7 KIA and 10 WIA. Three nights ago, we were down in the An Lao Valley on a night ambush and ran into four VC. We killed one and got his weapon and ended up spending the night in a rice paddy in the rain. That radio really gets heavy. It is really rough in the mountains, which we have been in for two days now. Sometimes, we can only see a few feet ahead of us. I am alright, except really tired, a heat rash and jungle rot on my feet. Hope everyone is well. Write more later.

Love,

Wayne

19 May 67

1636 hr S3 to C Co: start getting in a PZ posture your entire element will be going into BS 794252.

1705 hr C Co to TOC: <u>1st lift off the ground at this time enroute to BS 794252.</u>

1722 hr C Co to TOC: <u>1st lift on the ground at 1721 at BS 794252.</u>

1725 hr C Co to TOC: <u>lift these ships are dropping us from about 12-15 ft from the ground, have one man with a sprained back, also these ships are receiving sniper fire.</u>

1742 hr C Co to TOC: <u>C Co lift complete at this time.</u>

SUMMARY

C Co continued its search and destroy operations in the northern Bn AO until 1636 hrs when entire element was alerted to combat assault at 1705 hrs into BS 794252 and they TD at 1742 hrs. **The element was combat assaulted into position to reinforce for A Co and form a blocking position.** Initial combat assault into LZ resulted in 1 US WIA from enemy fire into helicopter. C Co was under sporadic sniper fire until 1830 hrs. **Element maneuvered in force to BS793253 to support A Co with any fire power needed, and block enemy ex-filtration to the W, NW and SW.** At 1830 hrs the 2d Plt of C Co 1-7 Cav was OCA to C Co 5-7 Cav. Element closed into BS 792246 in a blocking position.

18 May 67

0025 hr C Co to TOC: time 0015 location BS 764121 36A came in contact with 10-12 VC, VC walked into 36A ambush, 36A initiated contact, received incoming carbine fire, possibly AK-47 fire, believed to have killed 2 VC, appeared to have been wearing khaki's. Artillery called in at this time, VC were traveling from the south when hit, they ran across the fields to the west towards the hills.

0159 hr C Co to TOC: C Co reports that the area in which 36A had contact at 0015 is very thick with vegetation, will check it out at first light.

0655 hr C Co to TOC: follow-up of 36A contact last night at BS 735112 found one pack VC type, inside of pack were: black PJ's, green khaki's, shirt, medical aid packet, entrenching tool VC type, in same area found 2 Chicom grenade, one Russian light MG SN 502881, blood trail going SW to hills, drag marks indication one VC KIA, est 2 VC WIA, also found a diary, **36B found 1 VC KIA, wearing black shorts, gray khaki shirt, one German Mauser (Chicom copy) SN F1926, still searching the area.**

0936 hr C Co to TOC: for lift today will need 20 sorties of aircraft with an ACL of 6 PZ at BS 735125, LZ at BS 796284.

1030 hr C Co to TOC: location: BS 745119, center of mass.

1945 hr S3 to TOC: MED EVAC could not get into C Co location, will try later.

2130 hr To MED EVAC from TOC: request to get the man from C Co out now, believe ship can get in at this time.

2340 hr C Co to TOC: MED EVAC complete at this time.

SUMMARY

C Co at 0015 hrs vic BS 764121 made contact when 36A ambush patrol ambushed 10-12 VC; contact broken almost immediately when enemy fled to the west – estimate 2 VC KIA. Artillery was called in and saturated area of fleeing enemy with negative assessment. At 0600 hrs recon of the 2 contact areas (36A & 36B's locations) revealed the following: 36A – (BS 764121) 1 VCKIA (BC), 2 Chicom grenades, 1 Russian light MG, 1 VC pack, medical aid pack, and blood trail and drag marks along with 1 diary. Estimate 2 VC WIA, 36B (BS 735112) contact made at 171935: **1 VC KIA (BS), 1 Chicom type wpn,** estimate 1 VC WIA. C Co combat assaulted at 1519 hrs into LZ HORSE (BS 798284) with TD at 1550 hrs; they secured the LZ with negative enemy contact. They closed BS 799286 with 2 ambush patrols.

May 24, 1967

Dear Mom and Dad,

Hi! I will write a few lines now as I have some spare time. We have been in the mountains now for the last six days and are on top of a mountain cutting a LZ, which may take three days to do as it is really thick up here. The engineers are doing it while we secure it. I have not gotten any mail in a long time, but they have not been bringing much out here either. Did you hear about the peace truce they had over here yesterday? Do not believe it as the fighting went on the same as always. How are things at home? I'm still radioman and like the job, but it gets heavy sometimes. Are you sending me the **Western Kansas World?** *How did Chuck do in his final tests? How does Ron like being out of school now? Have they found summer jobs yet? Well, cannot think of much more, so will close for now.*

Lots of love,

Wayne

The peace truce I am referring to in my letter home was a military stand-down, which did occur on Buddha's birthday, May 23, 1967.

May 25, 1967

Dear Dad,

I sure was glad to hear from you today. It sounds like you are busy with irrigation and all. How do you like the new tractor? How does the wheat look this spring? I sure hope it turns out real good, as it has been a long time since you have had a good harvest. Today, we made a combat air assault into a little valley about one mile from the South China Sea. I was on the first helicopter into it, so they really cut loose with the machine gun before we landed. Tomorrow, we are going to the top of another mountain, close to here and be a blocking force for troops down on the Bong Son Plains, as there has been a lot of VC in there lately. I was just thinking of the Christmas present I could get you and mom, if you could use it. I could get you a real nice movie camera cheap. How did you like the pictures I took with my 35mm? It is too big to carry in the field, so sent it back in and am going to get a 104 for $10, which takes good slides to carry out here. If you will send some 8-cent stamps, I will send some more film home of pictures I took out here, but you will have to have them developed, as I do not know the address to *send it to, but will not cost you anything anyway. I am being careful, but have to do some things as this company came over here last summer and will be going home soon. That makes me an old guy now, so have to show some leadership for the new guys. I like the job of RTO. Well, it is about dark and I have guard first tonight, so will close for now.*

With love

Your son,

Wayne

Author digging a foxhole on the Bong Son Plains.

NVA Says Viet Cong

Torture Too Much

By PFC Roy O'Neal

A North Vietnamese Army soldier surrendered near Bong Son because he said he was disillusioned with the Viet Cong and their torture tactics.

He said he was attached to the 7th Battalion, 22nd North Vietnamese Army Regiment and had been working with it the past two years.

The night before he surrendered, he had succeeded in evading a Cavalry ambush. He had been in a shack with two friends when Cavalry men pounced upon them. His friends were killed, but he managed to escape.

He voluntarily surrendered the next morning. He said he would have surrendered sooner, but had been told that he would be shot by the Americans if he did so.

The soldier said he was weary of the Viet Cong treatment of the Vietnamese who refused to cooperate or join the communists. He said they were tortured, usually so severely that they would be lifetime invalids.

(Author's note: I cut this article out of a newspaper and sent it home in one of my letters)

Ken Baldwin gives his account of hitting the booby trap that day

(Transcribed from taped interview)

"I was back with C Company, 5th Battalion 7th Cavalry after spending my first month in-country assigned to an LRRP (Long Range Reconnaissance Patrol). On that morning, our company was moving from the An Lao Valley down onto the Bong Son Plains.

"Our platoon had point that day and the grunt who was supposed to walk point was a little disgruntled because he was due to leave for in-country R & R the next day. I volunteered to walk point for him. We were going downhill and as I rounded a bend in the trail, I saw the tripwire, but couldn't stop. The wire looked like fishing line as I tripped it. I hollered, 'Booby trap!' It seemed like everything was moving in slow motion as I turned around and everybody was running back up the trail.

"I took off running

MAY 28

Dear Mom + Dad,

My platoon has been here on the Bong Son Plains as a blocking force for the last two days so haven't had much to do for the last few days. It seems like it's been hotter than ever lately. Yesterday morning to we were moving down a trail when one of the guys in my squad hit a vc booby trap. He wasn't hurt to bad but had to be taken in by helicopter. He's from Lawrence, Kansas and we went through AIT and came over here together. How is everyone back home? I'm doing alright so far. Can't think of much more for now so will close. Write!

Love, Wayne

back up the trail also, which was the wrong thing to do. If I'd have just hit the ground, it would have blown over me and I would not have been wounded at all. It was actually behind me and was set up not to get me, but whoever was behind me. Generally, many of the times, you have the point man and then two or three guys back will be the sergeant. I was running up the hill out of the safe zone into the kill zone and was running out of it again when the booby trap explodes, hitting me in the leg.

"I could not run anymore, so I got over in the bushes by the trail and everything got very quiet. I remember someone hollering out, 'Is anybody hurt?'

"'Yeah,' I said.

"'Who is hurt?'

"'I am.'

"'How bad?'

"'I don't know.'

"'Well, can you walk?'

"'I don't know, I haven't tried.' The area was then secured and a MED EVAC helicopter was called in to take me to a field hospital. From there, I was transported to the hospital in Qui Nhon for surgery. I was then transferred to Okinawa for rehabilitation and then was sent back to my unit in the field."

27 May 67

0620 hr C Co to TOC: <u>request **MED EVAC for one man who walked into a booby trap, received shrapnel in the leg and buttocks, location BS 830225.**</u>

0725 hr C Co to TOC: <u>**MED EVAC complete at this time.**</u>

0730 hr C Co to TOC: <u>**the type of grenade used in the booby trap was Chicom, was set off by a trip wire.**</u>

0800 hr C Co to TOC: follow up report to finding 4 VC KIA (BS) at BS 815237, found 2 more VC KIA (BC), a total of 6 VC KIA (BC), 3 dressed in khaki uniforms, 3 in a lighter green clothing, one ruck sack, one pistol belt with poncho, gas mask, 2 canteens with covers, VC type, 110 rounds of AK-47 ammo, 3 small sacks of rice, 3 entrenching tools with covers, VC type, one roll of 7.62 ammo for machine gun, one chicom grenade, 4 sets of khaki clothing, 2 hammocks, one radio size 8x12x6, 2 band watt, SN 55-077-01, 2 SKS rifles SN 64187, and 7061222, documents hand written, and ID cards.

1146 hr C Co to TOC: time 1145 at BS 815237 on the NW side of knoll while checking out trail found tire tracks, first aid packet, blue sack, fire extinguisher (CO2 nitrogen type) cook pot, this trail appeared to have been an avenue of approach on the NE side of knoll. Patrol 11 found tire track VC, followed them until they faded out, then found a cave complex at BS 813238, C Co will keep us advised on the situation.

1340 hr C Co to TOC: reference spot report turned in at 1146H tire tracks were headed NW, negative finds in the cave complex.

SUMMARY

C Co continued blocking mission along TF Oregon Boundary Line with light enemy contact. **0650H the 3d platoon received one friendly WIA from an enemy booby trap while moving to C Co CP location (BS 815237), while checking area of contact (Ref FOR #146).** Also found 2 SKS rifles, one Chicom 2 watt radio, 110 rounds AK-47 ammo, 1 roll of 7.62 MG ammo, one Chicom grenade, and numerous smaller items. 1145H 1st platoon found vic BS 815237. Vic BS 813238 the 11 element found a fresh trail and bunker complex, searched area with negative assessment.

June 1, 1967

Dear Mom and Dad,

I will write you a few lines this evening before darkness sets in, but may be a few days before I can mail it, as we are in the mountains now. I received a letter from you yesterday and was sure glad to hear from you. It seems like the mail comes few and far between. I still have not received the World yet. Well, by next week, I will be down to 299 days left over here. Sometimes, time really goes fast and than other times slow. This is my 6th week over here in the field. I do not think we are going into An Khe until July or August, if then. How is everything going back home? What's Chuck doing this summer? How about Ron? We may be going up to LZ Sandra in a few days. I sure hope so. I never know what is happening around here from one day to the next. Well, cannot think of much more for now, so will close. Please write!

Lots of love

Your son,

Wayne

June 6, 1967

Dear Mom, Dad and Brothers,

Guess I will write a few lines this morning. We are on LZ Sandra and have been for the last three days. Yesterday, my platoon went out and we fired our weapons all afternoon. My M-16 kept jamming up and never did fire right, so am trying to get it fixed today. That rifle really makes me mad and I was just thinking that if we had gotten in a fire fight last week, I would have been in a world of hurt. I am no longer in the 1ˢᵗ squad of 3ʳᵈ platoon, but headquarters squad of 3ʳᵈ platoon now and a RTO and usually follow the lieutenant or platoon sergeant around. How is everyone doing? Well, I got a letter from Roger, Connie, a girl in Hays, and Mary, so had better get busy and write them. Write soon. I am still doing fine and in good shape. I just hope I can stay that way.

Lots and Lots of Love

Your son,

Wayne

May 23, 1967

Congressman claims M-16 is defective

A public controversy over the M-16, the basic combat rifle in Vietnam, began after Representative James J. Howard (D-New Jersey) read a letter to the House of Representatives in which a Marine in Vietnam claimed that almost all Americans killed in the battle for Hill 881 died as a result of their new M-16 rifles jamming. The Defense Department acknowledged on August 28 that there had been a "serious increase in frequency of malfunctions in the M-16."

The M-16 had become the standard U.S. Army infantry rifle in Vietnam earlier in 1967, replacing the M-14. Almost two pounds lighter and five inches shorter than the M-14, but with the same effective range of over 500 yards, it fired a smaller, lighter 5.56-mm cartridge. The M-16 could be fired fully automatic (like a machine gun) or one shot at a time.

Because the M-16 was rushed into mass production, early models were plagued by stoppages that caused some units to request a reissue of the M-14. Technical investigation revealed a variety of causes for the defect, in both the weapon and ammunition design and in care and cleaning in the field. With these deficiencies corrected, the M-16 became a popular infantry rifle that was able to hold its own against the Soviet-made AK-47 assault rifle used by the enemy.[8]

(Author's note: The above is a newspaper article.)

June 8 67

Dear Mom + Dad,

Just a few lines before it gets dark. We are on LZ Sandra now and I think tomorrow we are making an air assult on punji stake hill. Today we had two men wounded by punji stakes. Remember I told you I had traded my M-79 & .45 for his 16. Today I heard that he had been killed. I am sending a couple of pictures back I had taken here on LZ Sandra. I believe we are leaving here LZ Sandra to the An Lao Valley June 10. Well cant think of much more to say but just let you know I'm still ok. Hope everyone is ok. Write

Love, Wayne

Punji stick

The Punji stick or Punji stake is a type of a non-explosive booby trap. It is a simple spike, made out of wood or bamboo, generally placed upright in the ground. Punji sticks are usually deployed in substantial numbers.

Punji sticks would be placed in areas likely to be passed through by enemy (American) troops. The presence of punji sticks could be camouflaged by natural undergrowth, crops, grass, brush, or similar materials. They were often incorporated into various types of traps; for example, a camouflaged pit into which a man might fall.

Sometimes a pit would be dug with punji sticks in the sides pointing downward at an angle. A soldier stepping into the pit would find it impossible to remove his leg without doing severe damage, and injuries might be incurred by the simple fact of falling forward with one leg out, immobilizing the victim's unit longer than if the foot were simply pierced, in which case the victim could be evacuated by stretcher or fireman's carry if necessary.

Punji sticks were sometimes deployed in the preparation of an ambush. Soldiers lying in wait for the enemy to pass would deploy punji sticks in the area where the surprised enemy might be expected to take cover, thus soldiers diving for cover would impale themselves.

The tip of the punji stick was frequently smeared with feces, poison, or other contaminants to promote infection in the wound.

In the Vietnam War, the Viet Cong would also use this method to force the wounded soldier to be transported by helicopter to a medical hospital for treatment. Punji sticks were also used in Vietnam to complement various defenses, such as barbed wire.[9]

Punji stake field in Vietnam.

June 9, 1967

Dear Dad,

Received your letter today and was sure glad to hear from you. I am sending a roll of film home and all you have to do is send it into the company and they will send it back to you. It should not cost anything. Sounds like you have a lot of work to do now. Glad to hear the wheat is turning out ok. My platoon made a combat air assault today. I am RTO for the lieutenant and am doing real fine and being as careful as I can. I know that someday it will be my turn to come home. That is what keeps me going. Now that I have been over here for awhile, I am beginning to realize what life is all about and know how much I have to live for. Well, guess I had better close for now. Please write soon.

With love,

Wayne

Air Assault

Air assault is the movement of ground-based military forces by vertical take-off and landing (VTOL) aircraft – such as the helicopter – to seize and hold key terrain which has not been fully secured, and to directly engage enemy forces. In addition to regular infantry training, air-assault units usually receive training in rappelling and air transportation, and their equipment is sometimes designed or field-modified to allow better transportation within aircraft.

Due to the transport land restrictions of helicopters, air assault forces are usually light infantry, though some armored fighting vehicles, like the Russian BMD-1 are designed to fit most heavy lift helicopters, which enable assaulting forces to combine air mobility with a certain degree of ground mechanization. Invariably the assaulting troops are highly dependent on aerial fire support provided by the armed helicopters or fixed wing aircraft.

Air assault should not be confused with air attack, air strike, or air raid, which all refers to attack using solely aircraft (for example bombing, strafing, etc).

Moreover, air assault should not be confused with an airborne assault, which occurs when paratroopers, and their weapons and supplies, are dropped by parachute from transport aircraft, often as part of a strategic offensive operation. Air assault should not be also confused with forms of military transport operations known as air landing, airlift, or air bridge, that all require an already-secured place to land – an airhead.[10]

June 15, 1967

Dear Mom and Dad,

I will write a few lines this evening before it gets dark. We left LZ Sandra last Sunday and have been in the mountains ever since. I am head RTO now, so am walking with Lt Lytle. Now I have ringworm all over my left foot and cannot seem to get rid of it. If you know of something that will help, please send. I also need more paper and envelopes and try to send the self-sealed envelopes, as the others stuck together and was no good. I can also use any kind of food that you would want to send. One thing that I really am going to need is a rain suit, as it rains a lot and it really gets cold when it rains, believe me. By now, it must sound like I need a lot of things, but it would sure help if you would send those things.

Well, I cannot think of much more for now, so will close. Hope everyone is ok!

With love,

Wayne

June 20

Dear mom & Dad,

Well this really seems to be a way to pass the time by fast and helps me to stay awake on guard so am writing you a letter by the moon light. This is really a peaceful night if it would just stay like that. How's every thing at home now a days? I figure I've just about put in ¼ of my time in over here already. We are about to the An Lao Valley now. We killed a NVA officer today. Have you started cutting wheat yet? Will can't think of much more so will close for now.

Lots of love, Wayne

June 20, 1967

Dear Chuck and Ron,

Will try and write you guys tonight, as I am on guard duty now until midnight and there is a full moon out, so there is enough light to write by. What's been happening lately? Have there been any dances or anything like that lately? What did you do on your birthdays? HAPPY BIRTHDAY at any rate, anyway. Right now, we are at the northern edge of the An Lao Valley, but might make a combat air assault someplace tomorrow. I took some pictures from a helicopter during a combat air assault last week, so will send them home as soon as possible. Write sometime.

Your Brother,

Wayne

20 June 67

1035 hr C Co to TOC: C Co has contact with one VC. believe they got him, are sweeping the area at this time.

1045 hr C Co to TOC: fired at the one man who was running after searching area found man along with 6 children, persons are Montagnards, location BS 677235.

1058 hr C Co to TOC: follow-up report: have 7 children ages ranging from 2-15 yrs, one man about 40 yrs old, one woman. Found 2 T-shirts, one OD and one was white, 1 set of U S fatigues, one fatigue shirt with the name OBERY over the right pocket US Army on left pocket, also one plastic bag with 50 rounds of assorted M-16 & M-14 ammo.

1100 hr C Co to TOC: request MED EVAC for one man with extreme gastrointestinal pains, location at BS 677235.

1154 hr C Co to TOC: MED EVAC complete at this time.

1255 hr C Co to TOC: **time 1240 at BS 678233 right flank element spotted individual, he started to run, results one VC KIA dressed in khaki's.** Found in his possession a map of the An Lao Valley with positions marked on it. Also some other documents, this individual was carrying a pistol belt with a German Lugar type pistol.

1925 hr C Co to TOC: **reference 1 VC KIA by C Co: was carry a cigarette lighter with engraving "RODERICK – 5th Special Forces Group", 1st Special Forces Group, was also carrying one GI type belt and one garrote.**

SUMMARY

C Co continued search and destroy operations in the SONG DINH Valley with light enemy contact. At 1035H vic BS 677235, C Co detained 9 individuals including one man 40 yrs old, one women, and 7 children ranging in age from 2-15 yrs. All detainees were evacuated to LZ SANDRA for interrogation. At the same location, C Co also found 2 undershirts, one set of U.S. fatigues with the "OBERY" over the right pocket and a plastic bag containing 50 rounds of assorted M-16 and M-14 ammo. At 1100H vic 667235, C Co completed the MEDEVAC of one man suffering from severe gastronomical pains. **At 1255h vic BS 668233, C Co took under fire one individual dressed in khaki's and armed with a Walther pistol resulting in one VC KIA (BC).** From the maps and documents on the body, it appears that the individual was the district chief of the An Lao Valley. Individual was also carrying a cigarette lighter engraved with "Roderick, 5th Special Forces, 1st Special Forces Group" a GI belt and a garrote. At 1800 hrs C Co closed with 2 ambush positions at BS 660225.

Two members of B Co 1/7 Cavalry evacuate an old Vietnamese woman from the battlefield. Action took place during Operation Pershing. National Archives II file

CHAPTER EIGHT

The Ambush

June 22, 1967

Dearest Mom, Dad and Brothers,

Hi! They are giving us time to rest and take baths in a river this morning because of what happened last night. This is the most action I have seen yet, so guess I will tell you about it.

June 21, 1967

7:30 p.m. – My platoon moved into a little rice paddy just before night fall and set up an ambush about 50 yards from a well-used path. 9:30 p.m. – The 2nd squad spotted VC moving down the path towards our position. When they got in front of us, we blew three claymore mines and opened fire with two machine guns and all of our M-16s. I fired 120 rounds at them. When things quieted down, the platoon sergeant, three men and myself ran across the rice paddy to the path to get a body count and information off the bodies. We threw grenades going out there for our own protection and trying to get more VC. We found five dead, three men and two women. One of the women was carrying an M-1 rifle.

There was not much sleep to be had by anyone for the rest of the night. The next morning, we found one more dead VC woman and one VC man, who was wounded and had spent the whole night in a rice paddy, right in front of us. He was taken in by helicopter. It really was not a very pretty sight, but I guess that is what war is all about. I hope everyone is ok back home. Write!

With love,

Wayne

Every five minutes, one of the VC would blow a whistle. I suppose that meant "all clear," and the next group of Viet Cong would move down the trail. They would then move a little way and then stop, and one would go ahead to make sure the coast was clear. They would blow the whistle, and the rest of them would move on down the trail.

We had just been notified by the 2nd squad that the VC were headed down the path toward our position. Everything became very still as we lay waiting in ambush. My heart was pounding, my M-16 was switched to rock and roll (automatic fire position) as I held it to my right shoulder, finger on the trigger, and ready to fire.

I could barely see some dark figures in the distance, but as they drew closer, I could make out there were indeed some VC headed our way. When they walked in front of our position, all hell broke loose as we detonated the claymore mines and opened up with the M-60 machine guns and our M-16s. My adrenaline was flowing as I quickly fired off six-20 round clips of ammo at the Viet Cong.

After a few minutes, when the shooting died down, it got eerily silent. I wondered how many we had killed? How many more were out there alive? The platoon sergeant called for some volunteers to go out in the kill zone to check for dead Viet Cong. Being gung-ho, but very naïve about volunteering for such duty, I jumped up and joined three other comrades and the sergeant to go check the bodies out and recover any weapons, gear, or information we could find on them.

Illumination was called for, and soon the sky lit up as flares were tossed out of an Air Force C-123 plane circling overhead. We rushed across the rice paddy toward the path, stopping to throw grenades along the way. When we made it to the site of the ambush, we found five dead Viet Cong. The platoon sergeant wanted to make sure they were dead, so he ordered us to shoot them at close range. I could see that two of them were young women. One of them had a weapon, an M-1 carbine.

I will never forget looking at their faces, into their eyes as they lay there dead. They were so young and nice-looking, it really struck a chord with my conscience. The platoon sergeant talked about pulling down their pants. I thought, isn't this bad enough? I wanted no part of that.

The flare canisters were falling everywhere; no one knew where they were going to land. I could hear them coming down from the sky. One guy was hit by one of the canisters.

A few days later, our platoon was on patrol and we came back on the scene of the ambush. Their bodies were still by the path, just as we had left them. The heat and time had taken a toll—the remains were in a putrid condition. Maggots were crawling out of their eyes, ears, every place a maggot could crawl into. It was a very gross scene. The Viet Cong didn't police (gather up) their people up at all, they just let them lie.

21 June 67

0653 hr C Co to TOC: all patrols have closed at this time to CP location: (BS 660225).

1150 hr C Co to TOC: 16 element at 1030H found one hut and fresh foot prints in area, in hut found 100 new punji stakes, a butchered chicken and one pair of black PJ's at BS 655210, at 1030H at BS 656217 36 element found a CBU bomb, were unable to destroy it, at 1050H 36 element found 15' cave, could accommodate 6 VC, also in same vic found 2 old huts, cane and huts destroyed. At 1050H 16 element at BS 654212 found footprints of one person on side of the river bank, at 1030H 26 element at BS 667217 found and destroyed 2 old huts. At 1100H vic BS 673212 destroyed one old hut in same vic found a tunnel that went back 4 or 5 ft, could hold 2 VC found in tunnel an old metal ammo box, at 1120H at BS 649218 found fresh tracks and one hut, in hut found 20 NVA rubber sandals, also punji field of approx 200' in length, near hut with stakes measuring approx 2 ft.

1945 hr C Co to TOC: time 1940 at BS 655215 patrol 36 as they were moving into position spotted 4-5 individuals moving east – west, could not distinguish if they had weapons or packs. Patrol 36 will be around this location tonight.

2056 hr C Co to TOC: time 2050 at BS 65515 patrol 36 spotted 6-8 individuals took under fire, artillery going in at this time, have definitely spotted 10 persons, looks as though there is more in the area.

2110 hr C Co 36 element to TOC: have a lot of movement, no estimate of how many people, are setting up 2 blocking positions are engaging with mortars and artillery at this time.

2127 hr C Co 36 element to TOC: have received incoming hand grenades from the northwest, were thrown by confirmed NVA, **believe 5 VC KIA at this time.**

2136 hr S4 to TOC: emergency resupply ammo in-bound to C Co at this time.

2150 hr To TOC from all units: SITREP Green, **C Co still checking area, movement has ceased**, and resupply complete at this time.

2253 hr C Co to TOC: **in C Co kill zone have 5 VC KIA, 4 wore khakis either black or green, 1 VC wore white, color of uniforms hard to distinguish because of light conditions. Captured one M-1 carbine,** numerous documents, web gear, including 3 pistol belts, VC type, 3 canteens, 2 NVA hats, 3 leather belts, with buckles that have stars on them, 2 GT type duffel bags containing ponchos, cooking utensils, more documents, khakis and one wool sweat shirt, 3 cans cooked rice, and one whistle on a body, 36 element knows 3 VC escaped to NE towards C Co CP, 4 or 5 others went to SW. Artillery being called and C Co CO using VT, at 1st light will check area thoroughly for more KIA, ect C Co CO noted that when movement was taking place, whistle was blown at 5 minute intervals from flanks on the west and east of enemy position. VC element moving in unknown direction with whistles and miscellaneous noises from all directions, 36 element is to remain at present location.

2255 hr C Co to TOC: **SN of M-1 carbine is 1923807**, no friendly casualties, 36 element to stay at present location, VC may return to area to police up items left in the area, 36 element is well covered by arty, at 1st light a platoon will check out area and a platoon of C Co will join the 36 element for search and destroy, both elements VC force estimated to be 10-15 VC.

2306 hr C Co to TOC: scout ship will be ready to check the area around C Co at 1st light.

2310 hr C Co 36 element to TOC: have spotted more movement at est. 200 to 300 meters to front of 2-3 individuals, 36 fired on with negative assessment, illumination called and being used at this time.

SUMMARY

C Co continued search and destroy operations in the upper FISH HOOK area with light enemy contact resulting in 5 VC KIA (BC) and 1 weapon (M-1 carbine) captured, numerous items of web gear, clothing and documents. At 1940 hrs vic coord BS655215, the 36 element sighted 10 individuals; engaged with mortars and artillery. **At 2125 hrs, the 36 element received incoming hand grenades and returned fire killing 5 VC (BC) and capturing 1 M-1 carbine SN 1923807.** C Co closed with 4 ambush positions at BS 673215.

June 27, 1967

Dear Mom and Dad,

We were air-lifted yesterday out of where we got those VC and came to LZ English. The 173rd Air-Borne Division really got hit badly two days ago, so the 5th Battalion of the 7th Cavalry is going to Pleiku near the Cambodian border today. I guess we are going in C-130 aircrafts. The 173rd had 80 killed in action and one missing in action, so you can see why. There is a new fresh NVA unit there called the 24th Regiment, so could really be bad. They are also in the monsoon season up there, so I could use a light weight rain suit if you could send me one. How did the wheat turn out? How is Eddie doing in baseball? Those VC we killed the other night after the five of us ran out there, the platoon sergeant yelled, make sure they are dead, so I walked up and had to shoot them again at close range. That sure seemed cruel, but it did not seem to bother me like I thought it might. The next night, we set an ambush up in the same area. We spotted fifteen VC about 1000 meters away, so called in mortars on them. After it got dark, we had to cross a river. I fell down and got my radio wet, so it would not work at all and also lost my M-16 rifle. I found my rifle the next morning. Well, I will write more when we get to Pleiku and let you know what is going on. Please write soon.

Lots of love,

Wayne

July 1, 1967

Dear Mom, Dad and Brothers,

Well, nothing new has happened in the past week. We are still north of Pleiku on a LZ. Our platoon leader, Lt Lytle, got real sick last night, so had to go in. I may be transferred to headquarters and be a RTO up there. I sure hope so. I talked to the First Sergeant about it. Well, I suppose by now harvest is about over. How did it turn out this year? Have you gotten much rain lately? It rains here about every day. This is my fourth month over here now. My ringworm is getting a lot better now. I also had some on my hand. Well, I cannot think of much more for now, so will close. Please write soon.

Lots of love,

Wayne

July 4, 1967

Dear Mom, Dad and Brothers,

Hi there! How's everything been at home lately? Everything has been pretty good with me lately. My ringworm is about all gone, thank goodness! Yesterday, we were air-lifted a long way north and now am sitting on top of a mountain. We cut a LZ here today also. By the way, how did harvest turn out or did it ever dry up enough to cut? Did you finish drilling the milo and feed? Ever since that ambush on June 21st, it has kind of bothered me. I sure hope I never have to kill anyone again. I also know one more thing, I will never go running out in the open at night to see how many we killed, because there very well could have been more live VC out there who could have really wiped us out. It scares me to think about it now. Well, it's getting dark, so had better close. Please write soon!

Lots of love,

Wayne

CHAPTER NINE

Monsoon Season

July 10, 1967

Dear Mom, Dad and Brothers,

Well, I finally have a chance to write, so will try and write a few lines. Our old platoon leader, Lt Lytle, went home, so have a new one now, Lt Beck. I am his radioman. I am in my hooch now because it is raining out like usual. We are in the monsoon rain season up here where it rains day and night and I am always wet, muddy, and freezing, so has been rough lately. Yesterday, we came up to LZ Hastings. I got the rain jacket last night and other things. I was real happy to receive them. I slept in my rain jacket last night and it sure helped keep me warm. Did you get the wheat cut and hay put up? Do you plan on taking a trip later on this month or next? Well, I cannot think of much more for now, so will close. Thank you very much for sending the packages, as they really help a lot. I really look forward to getting packages and letters. I will write more in a day or so.

Lots of love,

Wayne

The Leeches

In Vietnam, not only did soldiers have to deal with an invisible enemy, but also the elements. The monsoon rain season runs from April or May to October. It was hard to stay dry, and it seemed like we were always wet, cold, and muddy. The dry season runs from December to April. Late February through May it is very hot and humid. The heat was hard to take, and we perspired a lot. Occasionally a soldier would develop a heat rash. I can remember one day while on patrol when I developed a rash on my neck and shoulders, making it very painful to carry my rucksack.

There were also a lot of bugs in Vietnam. There were mosquitoes, spiders, centipedes, scorpions, flies, bees and wasps aplenty. There were also ants, red and black, big and little. During the monsoon season we also had to watch out for leeches. I remember a particular incident when our company was camped on the side of a mountain in the jungle one night and it was raining as usual.

My buddy and I were sharing a small hooch (tent), trying to sleep on an air mattresses. Of course, being on the side of a mountain made it difficult to find a level place to lie down.

My comrade and I were trying to stay dry and get comfortable enough to get some shut-eye. I tossed and turned for a few hours, but finally fell asleep.

Sometime during the night while we were sleeping, the leeches found their way into our sleeping quarters. When I woke up the next morning, the first thing I noticed was that I could not see anything. I was blinded! I soon discovered that the leeches had attached themselves to my face during the night and my eyes were caked over with dried blood.

July 17, 1967

Dear Mom, Dad and Brothers,

Hi there! I received Chuck's letters today. Sounds like everybody is busy back home. Sorry I have not written more, but it rains a lot and am very busy. Made a combat air assault on my birthday and have been in a dense jungle area ever since. I am still head radioman and like the job. Boy, that rain suit sure is a big help. Did you ever get those color slides back? They were taken with a 104 and will take some more if they turn out ok! How did the harvest turn out? I am sending a picture of a car I want to order, except I want a 68. I am saving money, should have over $1000 *when I come home. I hope to make SP-4 in one or two months and maybe E-5 sergeant by the time I come home, so will mean more money. I would like to order it in December or January, so it will be there by the time I get home. I would also like to order it through the dealer back home, as the dealers over here cannot be trusted. Well, cannot think of much more, so will close. I am doing fine! Write!*

Lots of love,

Wayne

July 22, 1967

Dear Mom, Dad and Brothers,

The moon is out bright tonight, so thought I would write a few lines. It is midnight and am on radio watch. We are on a hill now and will move 2000 meters tomorrow and then supposed to be picked up the next day and go back to Kontum and from there, back to An Khe. We will be there three days and then go back to Bong Son Plains and An Lao Valley on Operation Pershing. Op Pershing started last February, so is really a long one. How is everyone at home? Has Chuck found a job? How's Eddie doing in baseball? Have you gotten the summer fallow done yet? How did my 104 pictures turn out? I am doing ok, but am a little tired. Cannot think of much more for now, so will close. They sure feed us poorly out here lately. Will write more back at An Khe.

Lots of love,

Wayne

Sometimes we did get some hot chow out in the field, but it didn't always taste good. Here is one memory of Ken Baldwin's: "Tonight the log bird was to bring us some hot chow. When we got to the chow line, the First Sgt told us we had to shave before we could eat. Lt Beck talked to the First Sgt and we got to eat unshaven. The next morning, before breakfast, Lt Beck came by and was clean shaven. He said if he

78

had to shave, we also had to."

July 29, 1967

Dear Mom and Dad,

Hi! Will write a few lines this evening. Have really been on the go lately which is why I have not written sooner. By the way, HAPPY BIRTHDAY Dad! We have moved back across the country by the South China Sea. We will be going to the An Lao Valley and Bong Son Plains in the next few days. Now, we are north of there in some mountains. Sure has been hot lately. My ringworm came back really bad this time, so am using the stuff you sent. Well, I have been out here in the jungle since April 20 without going back in. Sure seems like a long time and has been rough. I am still head radioman of the platoon. I work with Lt Beck. I have a cold and feel tired and run down, so will sure be glad when I get a chance to go back to the rear. We go on about four ambushes a week now. Sure hope I never see another Viet Cong! Well, have been in-country for 112 days, so have a long time to go yet. What's new at home now? Well, it is getting dark, so will have to close. Will try and write more often. It sure is a big help to get letters from home.

Love,

Wayne

Charles Spencer, left, and Lt. Winfield Beck, right.

Happy BIRTHDAY   July 31

Dear Dad,

Hi. Guess this will be late for your birthday but haven't had much time to write lately. I'm sitting here in a rice paddie now and have some free time. At 3 o'clock this afternoon we are being air lifted up to LZ Sandra but don't know how long we'll be there. I went down to a little river near by this morning and took a bath + shaved. Sure feels good to get cleaned up for a change. Well I start my 5th month over here tomorrow. How is everything at home? I still have some more letters to write and had better clean my rifle so will close. Love Wayne

August 3, 1967

Dearest Mom, Dad and Brothers,

Guess I will write a few lines this evening. We are set up for the night. We have been on ambushes for the last three nights. Three days ago, we made a combat air assault off of LZ Sandra. They gave us C rations enough to last three days to carry, so made my pack heavy. We have not had any hot chow or mail in a long time either. Dad, I guess tomorrow is your birthday, so HAPPY BIRTHDAY! This is short, but it is getting late, so will have to close. Please write soon. I am still doing fine!

Love,

Wayne

August 10, 1967

Dear Mom and Dad,

I have some time this morning, so will write. <u>At one o'clock this afternoon, we are being airlifted out of here to LZ Dot.</u> Sure hope we stay there for a few days, as I need the rest and food. How are things at home? I got a letter from Becky today that said they had been down. I suppose by now the fair is on. Probably about the same as always. We sure have been making a lot of combat air assaults lately. A company got hit by the NVA two days ago, so went in to help them. It sure has been hot lately. I hope you can read this as I have infection in my finger, so is hard to write.

Love,

Wayne

10 August 67

0812 hr C Co to TOC: Time 0812 hrs at BS 376382 found 2 huts partially destroyed – huts contained a total of 750 lbs of unharvested rice. Rice is in difficult terrain and will be hard to extract.

1303 hr C Co to TOC: **2d C Co lift at 1255 hrs TD LZ Dot at 1303 hrs.**

1320 hr C Co to TOC: **3d TD LZ Dot for C Co.**

1330 hr C Co to TOC: **C Co complete LZ Dot this time.**

1610 hr C Co to TOC: C Co receiving fire from village SW at LZ SWITCH.

1855 hr All units to TOC: Final location: C Co LZ Dot, 26 LZ SWITCH.

2050 hr TOC to BDE: SITREP Green

August 11, 1967

Folks,

I received one of your letters today. Sure glad to hear from you. I know I have not written much, but has really been hard going. I am sending a note to Aunt Blanche, so please send it to her, as I lost her address. She sent me a box of candy. Well, hope everyone is ok. Will write soon again.

Lots of love,

Wayne

P.S. Would sure like some more cake & fruits!

August 18, 1967

Dear Mom and Dad,

Hi. Just a few lines this evening as it is starting to get dark. I have gotten lots of mail lately. Most of them are 16 to 19 year old girls from Kansas. I am writing one girl from Mesa, AZ who is 17. We are out in the jungle yet. Sure am getting tired, but am making it ok. <u>A VC sniper shot and wounded one man today. The shots sounded pretty close to me.</u> I am still the lieutenant's RTO. Hope everyone is well. Write!

Love,

Wayne

18 August 67

SUMMARY

C Co at BS 675275 at 0945 hrs, the unit found 1 hut 8'x14' and 1 poncho and canteen, all destroyed. **At 1134 hrs at BS 685268, the element received sniper**

fire resulting in 1 U S WIA. A Troop 1/9 Cav gunships and tube artillery worked the target area with negative assessment. The WIA was evacuated at 1157 hrs.

They Run Like Jackrabbits

One day, our platoon was working its way down the side of a mountain on patrol looking for Charlie (VC). As we neared the base of the mountain, we made contact with the enemy. It seemed like whenever we encountered the VC, they always seemed to be running. This phenomenon struck me as odd. It reminded me of the times when I was a boy hunting jackrabbits. They always seemed to be running. I did not realize the Viet Cong and NVA were totally dedicated to the reunification of Vietnam and willing to die for their country rather than surrender to the Americans.

On that particular day, I was following Lt. Beck, carrying the radio. We came to a trail along a hedgerow. I noticed some blood and a sandal. I excitedly informed the lieutenant, "I think they went that way!" The blood trail headed to our right toward some tall grass. We knew they were hiding in there somewhere. The lieutenant ordered us to make a U-shape formation and cautiously move forward. There were two enemy soldiers spotted in the distance. They would not surrender, so the platoon opened fire, killing one of them. The other one was lying on his stomach with his hands underneath him, still alive. No one wanted to turn him over for fear that he might have a live hand grenade.

While this action was occurring, the battalion headquarters had been contacted and wanted the enemy soldier taken prisoner. He might have some information that could be useful. All of a sudden, there was a loud pop and the VC was dead! Sam, the hippie from San Francisco, had walked up to him and shot him in the head, flattening his skull. Someone rolled him over and saw he was holding one of his sandals. It turned out that he was an NVA officer carrying a pistol. His legs had been shot full of holes. He had some papers on him that contained useful information about his unit and enemy troop movement.

One of the interesting things about Sam, the hippie from San Francisco, was that once a month his girlfriend mailed him a *Playboy* magazine. Inside the centerfold, she would tape some illegal drugs. Everyone had his own way of coping and trying to survive his tour of duty and come home alive.

While we were in Vietnam, the guys would try, when possible, to help each other out and make it a little easier for their buddies. Ken Baldwin remembers, "On my birthday, we set up our perimeter and settled in for the night, I celebrated with a can of pound cake and peaches. Then, as a present from the rest of the squad, I got the first and last guard shifts. That way, I got to sleep most of the night uninterrupted. It was a great present!"

CHAPTER TEN

Hospitalized

August 23, 1967

Dear Mom, Dad and Brothers,

Sure am sorry I have not written sooner, but have not been doing so well lately. I am at LZ English now at the 15th Medical Hospital. I gave my radio job up two days ago because of my leg and came in this morning. The company is on a high mountain now serving as an observation post overlooking the An Lao Valley. When I go back out, I will be a rifleman with the 3rd platoon, 3rd squad. The radio got too heavy, 30 lbs plus my pack made it over 40 lbs, so maybe you can see why. I forgot to tell you I have a pretty badly infected leg. I got some shots today and probably some more tomorrow. I think I am supposed to be here a week or so. It sure is nice to get out of the field, believe me! How is everyone at home? Guess it is about time for school to start again. This is about the end of my fifth month over here. Sure has seemed like a long time. Aunt Ruby sent me a package that sure was nice. I would really like it if you could send some fruit and cookies. I also need another rain suit, because the one you sent me is worn out. Maybe you can get a camouflaged one with lining inside, because the other one ripped too easily. Guess I had better close for now. They have a movie (outdoor-type) tonight here which is something new for me ha! And cold pop! Write!

Love,

Wayne

August 25, 1967

Hi Chuck,

Thought I would drop you a few lines this evening. I am waiting now to get my shots, three a day, but my leg is getting better anyway. Say, I read in the paper where you got caught speeding. All I can say is 'sorry bout that'! I really cannot talk, as I got one last year. This place sure is boring. I am ready to go out and shoot at the VC again. Are you ready for school to start? Is you car going to make it this year? Have you heard Dad say anything about me wanting to order a 68 Camaro? I am saving some pretty good money over here. I will talk to him about it later this fall. I can hardly wait to go on R & R in Tokyo or Hong Kong. Girls, Girls, Girls! If you, Ron or Eddie would like a suit or something when I go on R & R, send me your sizes, chest, waist length etc. and I might be able to get some real nice clothes for you cheap, tailor-made. They would not be wild either! I would like to get a stereo tape recorder, "Sony" also and send it home. I do not know whether you know or not, but from what I have heard, some of the best clothes in the world are made in the Orient. Well, really cannot think of much more for now, so will close. Take it easy in school! Be sure and send me your address! Write!

Wayne

August 25, 1967

Hi Ron,

I am on a letter-writing rage as I have got lots of free time now. All I have to do is eat and sleep! Are you looking forward to school this year? Guess what? I see the guy getting his needles ready. I sure am getting sore, about 15 shots in three days. By the way, are you going out for wrestling down there at Hays? If you do, good luck! If you are home some weekend when I go on R & R, I might get to talk to you guys. Sure would be nice. Where are you staying down at Hays? Send me your address! It is about time for my shot, so had better close. Write!

Wayne

It was a relief to come in from the field, even though I had to have a badly infected leg as the reason. At least I was in a place where I could enjoy hot chow, cold pop, and see a movie. Operation Pershing was now extending into its seventh month since the 1st Cavalry had started the search-and-destroy mission. I had been out in the field for about five months since my arrival in-country without many breaks, so coming into LZ English for a few days was a real treat. Having some downtime to rest and heal did wonders, because after a week in the rear, I was ready to go back out in the field and join my unit. I had become close to some of the guys in my squad, and I missed being with them. I felt responsible for them and needed to be out there to help my comrades make it through the bad situation we were in, so we could all come home.

A lot of things had happened in my first five months in Vietnam. I had gotten over being homesick in a far-away land. I had learned about a whole new country and culture and a different way people lived. I had learned such terms as Di Di Mau: move quickly; Dinky Dau: You're Crazy; Charlie, Charles, Chuck: Viet Cong, short for the phonetic representation Victor Charlie; Doc: what the grunts would call medics; Gooks was a slang expression brought to Vietnam by Korean War Veterans, the term referred to anyone of Asian origin; Heat tabs: fuel pellets used for heating C-rations; Mama-San: mature Vietnamese woman; Number One: good; Number Ten: bad; Papa-San: an elderly Vietnamese man.[11]

These are some of the events that happened during my first six months in-country that I clearly remember. One night we were camped on the side of a mountain, and, in the middle of the night, I awoke feeling really sick. I was experiencing terrible stomach cramps and was vomiting. Early the next morning, a MED EVAC (medical evacuation by helicopter: also called an "evac" or

"Dustoff")[11] was called for and I went back to the rear for treatment. I recovered in a few days and went back to join my unit.

One day, we were out on patrol looking for Charlie. We were moving along on a well-used path. After humping for an hour or so, the platoon sergeant decided it was time to take a well deserved-break. I needed to go to the bathroom, so I stepped into the bushes by the trail and disappeared out of sight. I didn't remember to inform my comrades where I was going. When I started walking back toward the path, my steps on the underbrush caused a crunching sound, alerting the others that someone or something was near by. When I emerged, the squad had their weapons pointed right at me, ready to fire. Boy, did that ever scare the hell out of me! The platoon sergeant let me know in no uncertain terms I was never to do that again.

Another day, we were out in the boonies, I remember a helicopter landed near our camp. Though helicopters landing near our camp weren't anything unusual, this one carried an unexpected visitor. The man walked toward us and the next thing I recall, I am shaking hands with none other than Charlton Heston, the famous movie star. When he took my hand in his large grasp, it engulfed mine. Mr. Heston had taken time to come to our encampment to show his support for the US war effort. This was a real morale booster and honor to have him come out in the field to visit us.

In retrospect, I have to wonder how we were winning the hearts and minds of the Vietnamese people. We were destroying their homes and food, killing their livestock, and making refugees out of them. It really did not make much sense. Of course, the purpose was to deny the Viet Cong a way to co-exist with the general population so that the communists could not continue their operations against the South Vietnamese people. Unfortunately, this strategy led to a lot of human suffering.

I had seen a lot of death in my first five months in-country. I had come to dehumanize the Viet Cong and NVA. Somehow, they seemed less than human. They were just gooks and it was okay to shoot and kill them. After all, they were trying to do the same thing to us. It became a matter of survival. All you wanted to do was just make it day to day and someday you would go home and everything would return to normal. The reality was that a lot of soldiers came home carrying the scars of war, both physical and psychological.

CHAPTER ELEVEN

Going on R & R

Sept. 1

Dear mom Dad & brothers,

Hi! I received your letter with the pictures. They were very good and really enjoyed them. I'm sending them back as I have no place to keep them along with one picture of myself taken at LZ English on the back of our supply. I came back to the field yesterday. We're at LZ Two Bits in the Bong Son area. It's the forward CP for the 1st Air Cav. We may stay here 10 to 15 days I think because of the elections coming up Sunday. We go on night patrols around here also. Well can't think of much more for now. Tell Eddie I'll be writing him soon.

your son,

Wayne

Author standing in back of supply room at LZ English.

September 11, 1967

Dear Mom and Dad,

Hi! Did you enjoy your trip? Where did you go anyway? I got your card. I also got Grandma's cake. It sure was good. Did you get me a rain jacket yet? I sure could use one. Guess what? Tomorrow we are going into An Khe and will be there for two weeks. I may try and call you. We can talk for three minutes and does not cost too much. Sure would be nice. I hope to go on R & R next month, so will get to talk to you then. This week, our platoon got into a fire fight. We killed 17 VC and we had one guy killed and three wounded. Today, the General gave our lieutenant and four other guys the Bronze Star with V device for that fight. We are starting to make a name for ourselves. How's everything at home? Well, tomorrow, I will have just 199 days left over here. Boy, sure will be glad when it's over. Well, guess I will close.

Lots of love,

Wayne

September 14, 1967

Dearest Mom and Dad,

Hi! I will bet you sure were surprised that I called. We were in An Khe for three days, so thought I would try and call. I waited 12 hours to get the call through, as they didn't have contact with the States all that time, but when they finally got through, I was the first one to talk. It was one a.m. here. My R & R starts September 19th – 26th, so will probably have called you before you receive this. I am supposed to go to Manila, but will let you know when I get there. Did they tell you, you had to say over before you talked to me, because you knew what to say? There were a lot of questions I wanted to ask, but didn't have much time and was kind of hard to talk. I have received lots of letters from girls in Kansas, so having a hard time keeping up with them. I really must go now. I get to go back into An Khe tomorrow to prepare for my R & R. Good bye.

Lots of love

Your son,

Wayne

September 17, 1967

Dearest Mom, Dad and Eddie,

Hello! Well, tomorrow I leave on R & R and am supposed to go to Manila, but am trying to go to Taipei. I received a letter from Chuck and Ron this morning. I am taking a little over $500 with me, so will be sending some things home. Will be kind of early, but will be sending you all Christmas gifts as will be the *only chance I have to get anything. Also, I plan on getting a Sony stereo tape recorder. I am going down there this afternoon and try and get my picture taken, as all these girls want my picture. Sure do have to write a lot of letters to keep up. Hope everyone is fine.*

Lots of love,

Wayne

R & R – Rest and Recreation vacation taken during a one-year tour of duty in Vietnam. The most popular destinations to take R & R were Bangkok, Hawaii, Australia, Hong Kong, Manila, Penang, Taipei, Kuala Lumpur, or Singapore. In-country R & Rs were taken in Vung Tau and China Beach, near DaNang.

September 25, 1967

Dear Mom, Dad and Ed,

Hi! I got back to Vietnam from Manila yesterday and back here to An Khe this morning. I really had a great time and plan on taking a seven day leave in January to Hong Kong or Tokyo. I didn't buy too much while I was over there, so am only sending home a picture. I picked up two cameras though, so now have three. I got a flash gun for my 35mm and got a 104 Polaroid Land camera, which is real small, so will carry it out in the field. The battalion is still in An Khe and will be moving south next month. O yes, the last night in Manila I called Dianne. The operator took WaKeeney for that city in Wisconsin, as I know you are probably wondering who I was calling in Wisconsin. I had a real nice talk with her. She has been writing me lately. Write soon!

Lots of love

Your son,

Wayne

October 1, 1967

Dear Mom, Dad and Ed,

Hi! Received your letter today and glad to hear from you. I wrote a letter to Mrs. Harvey at the high school. I wrote about the people and what it is like to be in Vietnam. I am number 1 in our platoon on the SP-4 list, so should make E-4 this month or next. It does not sound like the football team is doing very good this year. Is Eddie ok? It rains everyday now as the monsoon season is starting. Could you send me some writing paper and envelopes? I am about out. My ringworm broke out again and is a lot worse this time. I cannot seem to get rid of it. Well, I cannot think of much more for now, so will close. Hope everyone is fine.

Lots of love

Your son,

Wayne

An Lao Valley. A trooper and his dog with D Co 1/7 regiment 1st Cavalry Division, wade through a small stream during Operation Pershing.
National Archives II file

CHAPTER TWELVE

The Home Front

The American soldiers fighting in the Vietnam War almost all had family and friends back home—mothers, fathers, brothers, sisters, extended family, girlfriends, and buddies. War is hard, sometimes harder on the folks back home than on the sons and daughters doing the fighting. Did mom and dad ever get through a daylight hour without moments of dread, a feeling that something bad had happened to their loved one? What about the night? Did they lie awake at night worrying?

If a soldier is wounded, doesn't his mother feel the pain? If a son dies, isn't a part of the father's life taken away? No parent, husband, or wife wanted to hear the knock on the door and open it to see military personnel carrying the news that a son, daughter, wife, or husband had been wounded or killed in action.

Vietnam was the first televised war. Every evening, graphic images of the fighting, wounded, dying, and massive destruction were shown. Whenever the news about Vietnam came on, my brother Ed, who was a junior in high school at the time, would get up and leave the room. For those who had loved ones fighting in Vietnam, it was difficult to watch television. The war had a profound effect on families. The day after I left for Vietnam was really hard on Mom and Dad.

They found a distraction by visiting the neighbors to play cards. Mom said, "The next day after you left, it was really hard. The neighbors were good to cheer us up and help us through."

Dad said, "At the time we were developing an irrigation system for the farm, which kind of helped keep us busy."

"Other people were good too," Mom said. "Some of them had the same thing. We just kind of helped each other."

My Thoughts

By: Dianne Tegtmeyer Barnett

Small Town USA, where life consisted of church on Sunday, choir practice on Wednesday, Friday night sports, and families teaching responsibility, honor, and strong moral values. Saturday nights were reserved for teen dances at the local VFW with bands coming from as far away as Kansas City and Denver. Wow, wasn't life grand? Who could ask for more? My life at fourteen was great. A "conflict" halfway around the world in a place called Vietnam was simply unreal.

It was 1964 and I had my first romantic encounter. Walking down the halls of high school to a class that held no one's interest, I looked up and there he was. There was an innocent baby face with the most gorgeous eyes…my first glimpse of Wayne. He was seventeen, and I believed him to be the cutest boy I had ever seen. Believe it or not…he noticed me too. The school year held wonder for two young people discovering life and their feelings for each other. The year passed in a blur ending in graduation for Wayne. It was 1965 and the next phase of life and the realities of separation became a reality. Wayne left WaKeeney for Denver to begin a different life.

Being honor bound in the midst of a war that was consuming America, Wayne volunteered for service. Following basic training, AIT, and being deployed to Vietnam, the days passed and letters became infrequent. For me, small town life continued as normal. Knowing Wayne was involved in fighting for a cause I didn't understand seemed not to touch much of how I continued to view life. High school, church, studies, and my own looming graduation consumed my days. Sporadic letter writing and trying to keep letters light, in reflection, seems today to be so self-centered and unreal.

Television began bringing the war into our homes every day. One night while watching the news…there he was, Wayne. The face looked the same, but there was something different. His eyes…no longer the bright, tender eyes I had known to look at the world with wonder and caring. These eyes looked strained and discouraged. What had they seen? What had driven the innocent look away?

I began to watch more of the news for additional information. The images and stories brought forward along with the protestation of some of the population only led to me waking in the night shaking from an unknown fear. What possibly could this person I had known as an innocent boy halfway around the world possibly be enduring in a jungle along with other boys like him from all across the United States? If I felt this terror and fear from the safety of my little world, what must his everyday life be like right there in the midst of things?

One day at work, I received a call from Wayne. He was on leave in Manila and he sounded so tired. He informed me he was forwarding a picture he had taken there and I should be looking forward to receiving it soon. We had a carefree conversation for a short period because I was at work. Once again, the call invoked a wonder of relief that he was safe for a period of time. After a few weeks, the picture arrived and I was able to see Wayne in his combat gear. What a striking photo. The face was the same, but once again, the eyes were different.

I thanked God Wayne came home alive but wondered, at what it had cost him? Though he still looked the same, his eyes told a different story.

Returning home to a country that was involved in its own internal strife because of a war no one wanted or understood left him and countless others with their own unrest and internal conflicts.

I have heard it said that the eyes are the windows to the soul. If that is true, I believe Wayne's eyes told a story that I could not truly understand. Though Wayne and others were led to believe in honor, duty, and a country where freedom was taken for granted, many returned to only find a life of love interrupted, youth forgotten, and innocence lost.

Picture of author sent home from Manila, Philippines, while on R & R.

CHAPTER THIRTEEN

Moving North

October 1, 1967

Dearest Mom and Dad,

I have already written you today, but we got some news this evening that I thought I would tell you about. It does not sound very good. October 4ᵗʰ the battalion is moving north to Danang where the Marines are located. They are also in the monsoon rain season, so will make things worse. For the first time since I came over here, we will be wearing that vest to protect us from shrapnel and will also carry gas masks. Sure will be glad when these next six months go by. The first six went real fast, but time is starting to drag now. If I can get another rest leave, it sure will help. Have you got the wheat drilled yet? Sure hope it turns out good this year. This girl named Judy, who is a Sr. at Lawrence, Ks, high school writes me every two or three days, so am getting some mail. What do you think about me getting a new car when I get home? If I cannot pay for it, I won't, but I am trying to arrange and save my money so that I can buy a car. I am going to try and get out of the Army next August, so I can go back to school. I would like to go to school in Hays and take only seven or eight credit hours and work seven or eight hours a day. I believe I have learned how to work, as we work seven days a week over here, sometimes 24 hours a day. Well, enough of that. I must close for now as it is about dark. Write soon and I will be writing in a few days.

Lots of love,

Wayne

October 5, 1967

Dearest Mom and Dad,

Hi! Will try to write a few lines this afternoon. We moved north from An Khe three days ago and have been by an airfield ever since we got here guarding it. We are supposed to make a combat air, assault within the next two days. We replaced a Marine unit up here. It rains everyday. How is everything back home? Hope fine. Have you finished drilling wheat yet? Has WaKeeney won a football game yet? I have been here over six months now and have 177 days left. Still a long time. Guess I had better go now. Write real soon.

Lots of love,

Wayne

October 17, 1967

Dear Mom, Dad and Ed,

Hi! Sorry I have not written sooner, but some pretty bad things have been happening lately. Three days ago, the company got ambushed by a big NVA unit. We lost eight guys, one dead and seven wounded. They have us on LZ Colt now, securing the battalion CP. By the way, I made E-4 yesterday, so have a little more rank and money. I received a box of cookies from Aunt Blanche this morning. Sure was good. How is everything at home? We also had two guys go crazy in that last fire fight. I guess it just got to them, afraid that they were going to be killed. Sounds like Eddie is doing real well in football now. It rains over here everyday, so that rain suit sure comes in handy. My pen quit writing, so will have to use a pencil. I really cannot think of much more for now, so will close. Write soon.

Lot of love,

Wayne

October 18, 1967

Dear Eddie,

I have a few spare moments this evening, so thought I would write to you. How has everything been going for you lately? How about football? Our company has really been getting into fire fights lately. The shorter I get, the more scared I get. I am down to 159 days now and if I can make it for the next 140 days, I will have it made. I am so tired of being shot at and shooting at the VC, I do not think I will ever want to see a war movie again. How is school so far? Do they still have dances at the VFW? I am having to use a flashlight now to write, so had better close. I would like to hear from you sometime.

Your Brother,

SP-4 Wayne

P.S.   By the way, I made SP-4 this week.
That's about $35 more a month

October 23, 1967

Dear Mom, Dad and Eddie,

I was so glad to receive your letter today. Things have been about the same with me, we have been on LZ Colt since the 14ᵗʰ and I think we will be moving back to the field tomorrow. B and D companies are in a big fire fight now. There seems to be a lot more communists up here. I received a letter from Roger yesterday and he is in Washington DC now. He works for a two star General and lives in an apartment. Sounds like Eddie is doing real good in football. It has not rained much lately, but sure is hot. Well, hope this finds everyone ok.

Lots of love,

Wayne

CHAPTER FOURTEEN

Becoming a Forward Observer

October 30, 1967

Dear Mom, Dad and Ed,

Hi! We are just sitting around here this morning as we are making an air assault around noon. I have a new job now as a mortar FO (Forward Observer). I have a lot to learn about it yet, but think I can do the job. I have to be good on map reading for one thing. Whenever our platoon gets in a fight, it will be my job to call in mortars on the enemy and adjust the rounds. In the past two weeks, I have made it from PFC to SP-4 and from rifleman to FO, so am real happy about that. I have been thinking a lot about extending for six more months over here. I still will probably have to stay in the field until March, but after that I could get a job in the rear where it would be a whole lot safer. In April, I would get a free month leave to any place in the world. I could come home in that time, but it would be my chance to see part of the world. Paris, Rome, Japan or any place, plus another R & R after that. I would also make $1,500 in those six months. When I come home next October, I would be out of the Army, but it would mean I would not be home for 19 months. Write and tell me what you think about it. I *got a letter from Chuck yesterday, sounds like they are real busy. Well, I cannot think of much more for now, so will close. Hope everyone is fine.*

Lots of love,

Wayne

November 6, 1967

Dear Mom and Dad,

Sorry, I have not written sooner, but have really been busy lately. <u>We have this morning free as this afternoon we are making a combat air assault.</u> Being FO has really been keeping me busy. I have not called in any fire missions yet and am glad of it, as I need more practice on the map. This map is really hard to read over here. We get paid the 15th, so I am sending a money order for $100 back to you. It should be there by the end of this month. I will have another $100 home in January, so you can finish paying that note. Are you still getting my savings bonds and if so, what are you doing with them? How did the football season end up? It will not be long until Thanksgiving time. We will probably be out of here by then. Well, have some letters to write, so will close for this time. Write soon.

Lots of love,

Wayne

November 6, 1967

Dear Chuck and Ron,

Hi! Just a few lines this morning. We have some spare time. How's college been treating you guys? I'm an FO (forward observer) now. I really like the job. We're making a combat air assault today. I only have 145 days left over here now. I'm thinking about extending six more months over here. If I do, in April I get to spend a month in any free country in the world. I would also get another R & R after that. Do they still have dances back in WaKeeney? Well, really must go now, so will close.

Wayne

6 Nov 67

1303 hr C Co received 4 WIA (line #12, 19, 84 134,) MED EVAC requested, tail #450 completed at 1315 hrs. Individuals were standing around a trash fire when a canister was thrown in. Canister detonated.

1438 hr C Co 1ˢᵗ lift off TD LZ Green

1440 hr C Co lift complete, LZ Green

1500 hr Co C 16 element at AT889252 engaged 1 VC wearing black Pj's, had green uniform underneath, results 1 VC KIA. VC had bottle of pills on him.

1530 hr Co C 26 element AT896247 engaged 1 NVA, results 1 NVA KIA, wearing green uniform, carrying two pairs change of uniform, salt, first aid equipment, 2 NVA gas masks, Co C 36 element at AT 892252.

1533 hr Co C 26 element at AT896247 found 1 hut destroyed by ARA or AS. Found 5 male bodies-KIA from today, fd 1 AK-47, destroyed.

1550 hr Co C at AT896247 has 1 VC KIA wearing black Pj's, negative weapon.

1552 hr Co C element at AT895249 found a tunnel & bunker complex with fresh sandal track in the area will check when they get flashlights.

1730 hr Co C CP AT897250, slash 16-AT895245, recap 2 VC KIA, 1 NVA KIA 4 detainees, 2 males and 2 females. Location for 2 males AT893249, 1 male AT894246, 2 females AT893248, ARA 5 VC KIA.

1805 hr Co C 36 element fd at 1500 hrs, 500 lbs of rice, destroyed AT894251.

SUMMARY

Co C at 1302 hrs, the unit had 3 WIA caused by a canister thrown into a trail fire, which exploded. The unit conducted an air move to vic AT889251. It was a secure move, completing the move at 1426 hrs. At 1500 hrs the 36 element found a 500 lbs of rice vic AT894251. At 1508 hrs the unit detained 2 VN males and 2 VN females vic AT893248. Negative readout on them. At 1545 hrs vic AT896247 the 26 element found killed 1 NVA in green uniform with 2 packs of salt, 1ˢᵗ aid kit and a gas mask. At the same location found 5 bodies killed by supporting ARA and 1 AK-47 assault rifle which was damaged due to fire. At same location the unit also took under fire and killed 1 VC in black Pj's.

November 8, 1967

Dear Mom, Dad and Ed,

Hi! Just a few lines this morning to let you know I am doing ok. We have a patrol this afternoon. I am doing pretty good so far as a FO. How did the hunting season turn out? Were there many birds? I am still thinking about extending for six more months over here, but first I would like to hear what you think about it. I might be able to be a security guard in the Saigon area or something like that. It would be a lot more money than if I was back in the States for 6 months. Be sure and let me know. Will close for this time.

Lots of love,

Wayne

November 13, 1967

Dear Mom, Dad and Ed,

Hi! Not too much is new with me lately. I got a cake from Peggy, cookies from Audrey and Becky and candy from Luella. Guess it is not too long until Thanksgiving. Did anyone come to go hunting this year? We get paid in two days, so will send a money order as soon as I can. I am still thinking about extending over here. Hard to decide. I have been thinking about it for over three months. How is the weather back there now? Cold? Well, guess I better close for now. Will write more soon.

Lots of love,

Wayne

11 Nov 67

1105 hr Co C 16 Element 939258, found 1 AK-47 rd.

1215 hr Co C Element vic 940260, found tunnel complex with 3 compartments, 4'x2',4'x6', 4'x4', with sleeping quarters, tailor shop, Japanese sewing machine, 100 ft of grey and black cloth, will be sent back.

1410 hr Co C requests MED EVAC for 2 civilians hit by artillery frag, vic 951264. MEDEVAC # 453 completed 1430 hr.

SUMMARY

Co C at 1005H vic AT935263 found and destroyed 50 lbs of rice. At 1013H vic AT935263 an old woman informed the unit that 2 weeks ago there were a large number of VC and NVA elements in the area. At 1215H vic AT940260 the 36 element found a tunnel complex with 3 compartments, 4x4, 4x6, 4x4, sleeping quarters and a tailor shop, with a sewing machine, and 35 yds of gray and black cloth, evacuated. At 1545H vic AT957257, the 36 element found 1 NVA entrenching tool at the entrance to a bunker and several footprints, none over 48 hrs old.

12 Nov 67

0950 hr Co C moving out at this time.

1038 hr Co C at 947273, found 300 lbs of rice in a haystack, will destroy.

1425 hr Co C 36 element 965267 have 1 female age 21 yrs old, female is very sick, request MEDEVAC. MEDEVAC #453 complete.

SUMMARY

Co C at 1121 hrs vic 947287, the 26 element questioned an old man. He stated that the area was controlled by a VC village chief. He also stated that this village chief was still in the area. Also in the same area they found some gas masks and documents. These documents indicated that the village chief was still in the area. At 1200 hrs vic 943287 request for LN# 33 with a friendly frag wound. He was hurt when destroying bunkers. At 1425 hrs vic 965267, MEDEVAC for VC female who was ill.

Mail Call: Every soldier looked forward to receiving mail and packages (goodies) from home. It was a great morale booster and temporarily brought joy and happiness in the midst of misery. Reading about what was happening back home, helped keep soldiers going. On the other hand, some soldiers received Dear John letters making it even harder to carry on. They not only had a war to fight, but had to deal with the terrible feeling that their wives or girlfriends had decided to call it quits.

During my one-year tour of duty, I received many letters and packages from family, friends, and pen pals. One person in particular wrote often, keeping me up on what was happening back on the home front. News about high school activities and happenings around my old hometown was a source of comfort.

Decades later I came across some of those letters that I had managed to save and bring home from Vietnam. The following is an excerpt from a letter written by Dianne Tegtmeyer Barnett. More excerpts from her letters she sent to me while I was stationed in Vietnam are contained in later chapters.

November 14, 1967

Dear Wayne,

Guess it has been quite awhile since I last wrote you. School and work have really been taking up all my time. Last week-end was pheasant season and boy were we ever busy out at the café. Really ran myself ragged. I made a little over $50 in all. Really helps the old bank account. Not much has been going on around here lately. There are dances every once in awhile. We came in third in football this year. Guess that isn't too bad. Wish it could have been better, but if it's between third and last I'm glad we got what we did. Basketball will be starting soon and I really think we might do some good out on the court this year. Certainly hope so. We have to be good at something. Guess Karen and I are going to get together and make a bunch of candy and things to send to you and her boyfriend. Really can't think of anything else to send you for Christmas. If you need or want something, just let me know and I'll see what I can do about getting it for you. Well, I really should get to studying, if I want to keep those grades up. I'm still thinking of you even if I don't write as often as I should. Take care of yourself and write soon. I miss you and can't wait till you get home in March.

Love always,
Dianne

Nov 14

Dear Mom Dad & Col,

Hi! Just a few lines this evening to let you know everything fine with me. The monsoon has really been bad the last few days. We didn't get any chow at all yesterday because of the rain so you probly know how that made us all feel. We got some ice in on the log bird tonite and some pop & beer so that helps a lot.

There has been quite a lot of action around here lately. A helicopter got shot down and some fire fights. I sure am tired of staying out here. We haven't been on a fire base in over 20 days and will be lucky if we make it to one by christmas. I hope this finds everyone ok. Will write soon.

lots of love
Wayne

CHAPTER FIFTEEN

Thanksgiving 1967

Nov 22

Dear Mom Dad & C.D,

Hi. Just a few lines to let
you know I'm alright. The
monsoon has really been bad
lately. It rains day + night.
Tomorrow is Thanksgiving. Sure
hope we get some turkey out
here. I got your letter yesterday
and glad to hear everyone ok!
We got brand new M-16 rifles
last week. I sure like it.

Well I have 130 days left
now. Time really seems to
go by slow. We have been
in the field now for over 40
days. Not to mention the news
so will close. Write soon.

Lots of love,
Wayne

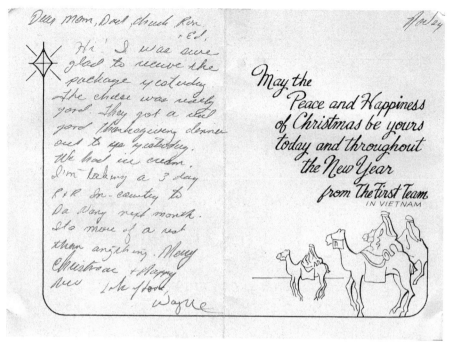

November 25, 1967

Dear Mom and Dad,

Hello! This afternoon we received some awards. Three of us got the Army Commendation Medal with V device. I am sending the orders with this letter and thought it would be nice if you would have this put in the Western Kansas World, as that way the people will know of some of the things we are doing over here. The reason and etc. is what you could have put in. It is really hot out this afternoon. How is the weather back there? When does the basketball season start? I cannot think of much else, so will close.

Lots of love,

Wayne

P.S. The package was just great! Be sure and do not lose those orders, as I may need them later on.

Leonard W Purinton Awarded Army Commendation Medal

Western Kansas World

December 1967

The following was received by PFC Leonard W Purinton, United States Army, Company C, 5th Battalion, 7th Cavalry.

For heroism in connection with military operations against a hostile force. Private First Class Purinton distinguished himself by heroism in action on 21, June 1967, while serving as a rifleman with Company C, 5th Battalion, 7th Cavalry during a night ambush in the An Lao Valley, Republic of Vietnam. On this date, one platoon of the company engaged an enemy force of unknown size which walked into their ambush. After the initial exchange of fire, movement outside the perimeter was detected in the vicinity of the enemy force. Private First Class Purinton, with complete disregard for his own safety, immediately volunteered to engage the enemy outside the perimeter. Accompanied by four other men, Private First Class Purinton, realizing the hostile soldiers were trying to escape and drag away their casualties, placed an intense volume of fire on the fleeing insurgents. His quick action prevented the enemy from escaping and accounted for six enemy killed. Private First Class Purinton's display of personal bravery and devotion to duty is in keeping with the highest traditions of the military service, and reflects great credit upon himself, his unit, and the United States Army.

Authority: By direction of the Secretary of the Army, under the provisions of Army Regulation 672-5-1.

November 29, 1967

Dear Mom, Dad and Eddie,

Hi. How is everyone by now? I am doing just fine. We have been on a fire base since the 23rd and will be making a combat air assault tomorrow. It has been raining most of the time for the past five days, so the helicopters have a hard time bringing in food. Did you receive my money order and about my medal ok? Sure would like it if you would send me some cakes, spice with icing and white *cake with icing. One of my friends got one yesterday and was still real fresh. I have gotten two fruit cakes and I cannot stand that kind. Did you write someone about sending me two rain-suits? I was called up to battalion HQ about it and cannot figure out what it is about or why? I am pretty sure I will not be extending over here after thinking it over carefully, as there are more bad points than good points. I do not know for sure yet, as it is still over three months off, but maybe I would like to have you meet me in Denver, as I may want to try and pick up a late model car 65-66. I will have between $600 to $800 to pay down. Well, it is starting to get dark, so must close for now. Goodbye.*

Lots of love

Wayne

NOTE: My father had contacted Congressman Bob Dole about my needing a rain suit. Congressman Dole then contacted our battalion in response to my father's inquiry. That was the reason I was called up to battalion HQ.

On patrol in the Que Son Valley, Quang Nam Province. The author is in front followed by Jesse Rodriguez carrying the M-60 machine gun, then Zygmunt Jablonski Jr., and bringing up the rear is Lee Danielson, squad leader. Jablonski and Danielson were later killed in action. Photo courtesy of Charles Spencer

CHAPTER SIXTEEN

Christmas 1967

December 9, 1967

Dear Mom and Dad,

Hi. Just a few lines this morning. We are making a combat air assault this morning, but it has been called off for one hour, so have some time to write. I am doing just great. Hope everyone is fine. I just thought of something. My driver's license expired last July. Did you ever receive a notice so I could renew it? If you did not, write the Motor Vehicle in Topeka and see if I can get one, as I will need it when I come home. I don't want to have to take a drivers test when I come home. Be sure and let me know as soon as you find out. I should have received a notice for renewal last June. Have you gotten much snow yet? It does not seem like December over here, as everything is green. I guess it stays like this year round. If you get a chance, see if they are still sending the **Western Kansas World** *to me, as I have not received it in a long time. Really cannot think of much more, so will close. Write soon.*

Lots of love,

Wayne

8 Dec 67

0800 hr Co C 1/6 ele vic BT172356 is in blocking force, 2/6 ele vic BT158373, 3/6 vic BT190360.

0844 hr Co C 3/6 ele policed up 1 M/A male with ID card, nothing suspicious. Request to know whether to detain him or release him.

0905 hr Co C 1/1 vic BT185355 spotted 1 indiv who was 100 meters right of the point man. He called for her to halt but she kept on going. 1/1 element fired a warning shot but she did not stop; results 1 VN female KIA. Female was 19 yrs old and was carrying a bundle of clothes.

0910 hr Co C 2/6 element vic BT165375 spotted 1 female 10 meters away and called for her to halt and fired a warning shot. 1 female WIA 25 yrs old and was carrying a bundle of clothes.

0915 hr Co C request MED EVAC for 1 civ female, who was 25 yrs old (WIA) vic BT165375. MED EVAC complete at 0925H.

0930 hr Co C 2/5 element vic BT171377 reports questioning 15 civ, who say VC went in all directions when 2/5 got near.

1030 hr Co C 2/6 element vic BT174360, has picked up 2 M/A males.

1258 hr Co C has a total of 6 M/A males. 2 have ID Cards. The location where the last 4 detainees were picked up at BT159361, will be evacuated.

1326 hr Co C foxhole count 131.

1530 hr Co C evacuation completed for their 6 detainees.

SUMMARY

Co C set up a blocking force vic BT152373 and BT172357. At 0905H vic BT185245, spotted 1 M/A female, they called for her to halt and fired a warning shot, but she continued to evade. The 11 element took her under fire; resulting in 1 VN female KIA. Indiv was carrying a bundle of clothes. At 0910H the 2/6 element vic BT165365, spotted 1 M/A female evading. The 2/6 element called for her to halt, she continued to evade and was taken under fire, resulting in 1 VN female WIA. She is approximately 25 yrs old and was carrying a bundle of clothes. At 1030H vic BT174360, the 2/6 element picked up 2 M/A males. At 1258H vic BT159361, they picked up 4 more M/A males.

In-Country R & R

December 10, 1967

Dear Mom, Dad and Ed,

Hi! Just a few lines as we just came back from a patrol. It has rained most of the afternoon, so am soaking wet, which is nothing new. I get to go in, in two more days for R & R in Danang. Sure will be glad, as I am tired of the field. This is short, but cannot think of too much more, so will close. Hope everyone is ok!

Write soon!

Lots of love,

Wayne

UNITED SERVICE ORGANIZATIONS, INC.
«A HOME AWAY FROM HOME» IN SOUTH VIETNAM
USO CHINA BEACH
FPO SAN FRANCISCO 96695

Dec. 17, 1967

Dear Mom, Dad, Chuck, Ron, & Eddie,

Hi! I'm in DaNang now and will be going back tomorrow morning. I'm at the USO now and have some time so will make this sort of a Christmas letter. This is a pretty nice place up here. You would'nt even know there's a war going on here. They have three big PX's here that have about every thing. Every night there's a floor show and movie. They also have good food which is really a change.

Has Wakeeney won any basketball games lately? When does college let out for the Christmas season? Will really can't think of to much more for now. Merry Christmas & Happy New Year as I will be thinking of you than. Write soon.

Lots of Love,

Wayne

USO MEMBER AGENCIES

THE YOUNG MEN'S CHRISTIAN ASSOCIATIONS. THE NATIONAL CATHOLIC COMMUNITY SERVICE.
THE NATIONAL JEWISH WELFARE BOARD THE YOUNG WOWEN'S CHRISTIAN ASSOCIATION.
THE SALVATION ARMY. THE NATIONAL TRAVELERS AID ASSOCIATION.
USO IS SUPPORTED PRIMARILY THROUGH UNITED FUNDS AND COMMUNITY CHESTS

December 18, 1967

Dear Mom and Dad,

Hi. Just got back from Danang this morning. I received your letter this morning also. I didn't know it was going to cost that much to call, or I never would have called her. I wanted to talk to someone was all, but when I get home, I will be sure and pay you for the one that cost $44. I put in for a six month extension over here to be in a security platoon, Saigon. It will take four to six weeks to be approved, but if not, then I will come home when I am supposed to. If I get the job, I will be home for a month in February. Believe me, it would be real good duty. I would live in a hotel. This is about the only way I can do it, so I will be able to pay back that bank note and still have some money left. I do not think I should try and buy a car while I am still in the Army, as it would be rough to pay for on Army pay and yet, if I was stationed in the States for my last six months, I would want a car, so maybe you can see why I am extending. In the end, I would come out ahead. If my extension comes through, I will be home for a month within the next two months. I received a package from Hollie's today. Well, really cannot think of much more, so will close.

Lots of love

Your son,

Wayne

P.S. Today, Bob Hope is in Danang, so missed him by just a few hours.

Landing Zone Colt
Christmas Day 67

Dear Mom, Dad, Chuck, Roo, & Eddie,

Merry Christmas! Hope you all have a nice day. It's cloudy and hot here today. We had a real nice dinner. I'm sending a menu with this letter also. What did you have for dinner? I'm really thinking of all of you today and wondering what you doing. Sure wish I could have gotten some gifts for you but didn't work out. Received a letter from Roger yesterday. Guess he's home for Christmas. It won't be to long until I can come home at least for a while. Write real soon.

Lots of love,
Wayne

Commander's Message

Throughout the Christian world, the Christmas season is a time of joy and spiritual inspiration. Despite separation from our families and the hardships imposed by war, those of us in Vietnam will still share the traditional Christmas spirit this year. We can enjoy the spiritual satisfaction that comes from giving. As fighting representatives of the Free World, our gift is the help we give the Vietnamese people to secure their independence, their individual safety, and their future freedom. Each of you gives a part of this gift and deserves the satisfaction of having increased the happiness of others – the true Christmas spirit. My best wishes to each of you and your families for the Christmas season. May you enjoy good fortune during the coming year.

W.C. WESTMORELAND

General, U.S. Army

Commanding

Prayer for Christmas

Our Father in Heaven, we give thee thanks for the gift of thy Son, Jesus Christ, our Savior, the Prince of Peace and Lord of Life. May thy gift of Bethlehem, announced by the Angelic Chorus, be born again in our hearts this day. Help us to know and experience the meaning and blessedness of their message: "Peace on Earth, Good Will Towards Men." Remove from us fear and hate and help us to know by faith thy peace which passes all understanding. We pray that the spirit of Christmas will be shared by our loved ones. With them help us to ponder, like Mary, the deep mystery of Christmas. May the truth and love which the Holy Child of Bethlehem brought to earth abide in our lives. In His name receive our praise and thanks. AMEN

Christmas Day Dinner

Shrimp Cocktail

Crackers

Roast Turkey

Turkey Gravy

Cornbread Dressing

Cranberry Sauce

Mashed Potatoes

Glazed Sweet Potatoes

Buttered Mixed Vegetables

Assorted Crisp Relishes

Hot Rolls

Butter

Fruit Cake

Mincemeat Pie

Pumpkin Pie w/ Whipped Topping

Assorted Fresh Fruits

Tea w/ Lemon

Milk

Assorted Nuts and Candy

CHAPTER SEVENTEEN

My Squad Leader's Death

"Greater love hath no man than this,

that a man lay down his life for his friends."

John 15:13

December 27, 1967

Dear Mom, Dad and Ed,

Hi! Just a few lines this afternoon to let you know I am doing ok. We are taking a chow break now in this village, as we are on a patrol. I received some packages from a high school girl in Delia and one from a girl in Lawrence. Also, I received a letter and picture from Peggy yesterday. The picture shows you, Ron, Peggy and kids and some old lady. I am anxious as to whether my extension is going to come through, but probably will not know until around the 1st of February. At any rate, it's only 95 days until I can come home. I really cannot think of much more. Write soon.

Love,

Wayne

January 2, 1968

Dear Mom, Dad and Ed,

Hi. I have some free time this afternoon as we just came back from patrol, so thought I would write. Received the letter that you all wrote at Aunt Becky's and was sure nice to hear from all of you. A VC walked up behind me this morning. I shot, but missed. I sure hate to let them get away, as that's just one more that might get one of us. How's the weather been back there lately? I suppose school has started up again. I believe I am right in extending over here. When I come home for a month's leave, I will be able to put $1000 in the bank and pay the rest of the bank note off and telephone bill. Duty in Saigon could be just as good as the States and will give me a head start after I am discharged from the Army. I will also get to see more of the world, as I would get two more R & Rs and could still save a $1000 more in that six months. It will not be as bad coming over here the second time as the first after being over here a year. I hope you can understand now why I am doing it. I still plan on finishing school at Parks. Well, had better close for now, so I can get this mailed. Write soon.

Lots of love,

Wayne

HAPPY BIRTHDAY!

Dear mom,

I'm writing this now as to make sure it gets there in time for your birthday. Hope you have a nice day and will be thinking of you then. I'm enclosing a poem that I've cut out of a paper. Just for you. Write soon.

Lots of Love,
your son,

Wayne

HAPPY BIRTHDAY!

MOTHER,

THE FORGOTTEN ONE

When soldiers are lonely in Vietnam

And their minds are full with

fear
They write I love you to their
girls
But forget the one most dear

I know your girl is wonderful
And fills your heart with joy
But your mother is the sweet
one
Who raised you since a baby
boy
Have you stopped and really
thought

How much she had done for you
For if so I'm sure you will know
She deserves your love most
true
Who has loved you since a tot

And cared for you all of your
life
I'm telling you dear soldier
It was neither your girl nor wife

So all us soldiers in Vietnam
Let's show our mothers we care
By writing them right today
And attaching this little prayer

Dear Heavenly Father up above
To my mother I send my love
I pray you bless this one so dear
And guide her thru the coming
years

Mostly Father I'm praying
That in the years to be
I find more ways of showing
Mom
How much she means to me.

PFC Lonnie Cherry

80th General Support Group

(Author's note: I came across this poem in a newspaper and thought it would be a nice gift for my mother's birthday.)

January 4, 1968

Dear Mom and Dad,

Hi. Just a few lines this evening to let you know I am alright. I am in my hooch writing this by flashlight. It has really turned cool the past few days. I do not want to scare you, but think it might be best if I tell you this. While we were on LZ Colt during Christmas, there was a pup that we played with some. A few days later, it turned out that he had rabies. I went in to see about the shots, but was told it was too late. I do not think it is anything to worry about as I am quite sure he did not bite me. I received a package from Sam's yesterday, but other than that, haven't received any mail this past week. Hope everyone is ok. Write soon.

Lots of love,

Wayne

Lee Danielson from Cadott, Wisconsin, was my squad leader who was killed that awful night on January 12, 1968. In the spring of 1990, twenty-two years after I came home from Vietnam, the Vietnam Veterans Memorial Moving Wall came to Ness City, Kansas. It was my first experience visiting the wall. It brought back a lot of sad memories. In the years that followed that first visit to the wall, as the anniversary of Lee's death (January 12) approached, I would become very depressed. By early evening on the anniversary day, I would experience periods of uncontrollable sobbing and intense grief.

Though I believed a piece of me had died along with Lee that fateful day, I remember wishing I could physically die and for once be at peace with the world. For years, I had thought about contacting Lee's family, but resisted reaching out because I was consumed by a fear of what would happen. Would I open up old wounds for the family? How would they react?

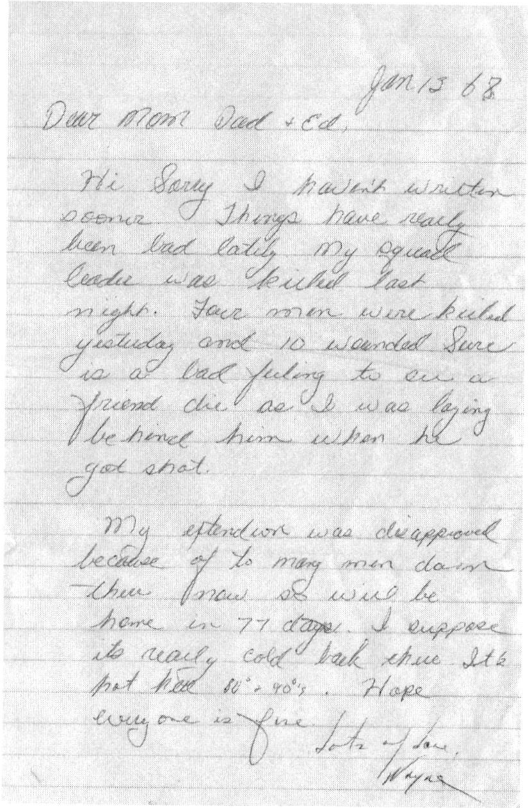

When the letters I had written home from Vietnam surfaced in June of 2000, I finally realized it was time for me to contact the Danielson family. In September 2000, I picked up the phone and called information to inquire if there were any Danielsons listed in the Cadott, Wisconsin, area, as I remembered Lee calling Cadott home. The first name I called turned out to be Lee's second cousin. This cousin put me in touch with Lee's sister, Jean. Jean had mixed feelings about talking with me and asked Perry, Lee's brother, to contact me.

When Perry called one evening, we ended up talking for about an hour. Lee's family had been waiting all those years for someone who knew Lee to call. I continued to remain in contact with the Danielson family through e-mails.

Handwritten letter:

Jan 13 68

Dear Mom Dad + Ed,

Hi Sorry I haven't written sooner Things have really been bad lately My squad leader was killed last night. Four men were killed yesterday and 10 wounded Sure is a bad feeling to see a friend die as I was laying beside him when he got shot.

My extended work was disapproved because of to many men claim there now so will be home in 77 days. I suppose its really cold back there Its not here 80's 90's. Hope everyone is fine

Lots of love,
Wayne

Author kneels at Lee Danielson's grave. Standing left to right: Perry, Jean, and Dan.

On Memorial Day weekend 2001, I made arrangements to travel to Cadott to meet Lee's family and visit his grave. Because of that weekend visit, I am now able to view January 12, the anniversary of Lee's death, with a sense of peace. I have come to realize that all those years, I had never had the chance to grieve for Lee. Each day the war continued and grief was replaced by survival.

THE CHIPPEWA HERALD

Chippewa Falls, WI, Sunday, May 27, 2001

Healing visit

Kansas man looks for peace at grave of Cadott man killed in Vietnam

By: Mark Gunderman (Mark received the Wisconsin Newspaper Association Foundation's first place award for feature writing in the *Chippewa Herald*'s circulation group in 2001 for this story)

Bullets shredded leaves on the trees and kicked up dirt on the ground as the NVA machine gunner bore down on the platoon of Americans lying in the small trench. Specialist 4th Class Wayne Purinton of Kansas had just crawled up to help his friend and unit leader, Sgt. Lee Danielson of Cadott. The shots that tore up the position in the next few seconds ended one life, and changed several others forever.

Through 32 Memorial Days since that fateful day of Jan. 12, 1968, Purinton struggled to come to terms with witnessing young Lee Danielson's death.

Through 32 Memorial Days, Danielson's brothers and sisters have honored the memory of Lee, still feeling the pain of the loss, each dealing in their own way with the still-lingering grief.

This year, they shared their memories and feelings together. Saturday at Brooklawn Cemetery in Cadott, Purinton and the Danielson family gathered at Lee's grave.

"I hope this meeting will help bring about closure for him and us," said Perry Danielson, Lee's younger brother, who was 13 in 1968. "Wayne will probably never know just how much it has meant to me that he has taken the risk of reaching out to us. It is hard for me to explain, but I do feel comforted knowing that Lee's death had an impact on some of his fellow soldiers."

Purinton said he told himself at the time, "Lee, I will never forget you and you will always be in my heart."

"The war went on, the expended being replaced by another expendable body," Purinton said. "In 1995 I began to feel the need to pay my respects to Lee and his family, something I never had the chance to do. Finally, in the fall of 2000, I decided to contact Lee's family."

Special son

Hearing from Purinton brought back both wonderful and painful memories for the family, which consists of brothers Perry and Darrell (known as Dan), and sisters Sharon (Hillestad) and Jean (Poehls).

"Lee was kind of a mild-mannered, easy going person," said Dan, who was born two years before and was in the Navy when Lee died.

Lee enjoyed farm work, taking care of the cattle while Dan took care of the machinery. "He was very much a manager type," Dan said.

The family is no stranger to tragedy. Their father, Ernest, suffered from mental illness and committed suicide in 1965.

"I remember (Lee) talking to me about our dad's mental illness. He was preparing me for what might happen," Perry said. When it happened, Dan and Sharon had already left home, leaving Lee, Perry and Jean with their mother, Margaretta. "I remember Lee as an incredible role model for me," said Perry. "He grew up real fast. He was just a real loving kid. He really took over a lot because our dad was sick for about seven years," Jean said.

Dan, stationed in Cuba at the time, approved of Lee's decision to join the Army. Lee saw heavy action. He would send pictures back to Dan, with instructions to keep them away from their mother. He didn't want her to know just how much action he really was seeing.

At age 20, Lee became the sixth Chippewa County man killed in Vietnam. His death made local news.

Battle scars

Lee was buried in Brooklawn Cemetery. Long after the war ended, the deaths continued to exert a powerful effect on many individuals.

When he arrived home in 1968, Purinton weighed only 110 pounds. "I was emotionally numb and could not talk to anyone about my combat experiences. I couldn't seem to take enough showers, and had a bad attitude," he said.

Purinton married, raised a family, and tried to farm. He lost the farm in the 1985 farm crisis and took a job at the county highway department.

In May 1990, he recalls the Vietnam Moving Wall came to a nearby town. "Visiting the wall and looking up the names of my buddies who had been killed was like opening up a floodgate," he said. "There were a lot of tears. I had been repressing my feelings about Vietnam for years and finally had to deal with it."

He looked for healing in a trip to Vietnam in 1994, returning with other veterans in 1995. "It was a positive experience and some healing occurred," he said.

He was diagnosed with severe Post-Traumatic Stress Disorder in 1997 and entered a 90-day in-patient readjustment program.

In November 1998, Purinton made a solo trip to Hanoi, visited an orphanage and is now helping to support a war orphan who wants to attend college. Both his doctor and his father suggested contacting Lee's family.

Family remembers

Dan Danielson had difficulty at first accepting the fact of Lee's death. "It was devastating for me," he said, "I was just numb for the whole trip back." He kept telling himself of a possibility of a military mix-up, but he identified the body at a Cadott funeral home.

"I can still vividly remember Darrell coming back home and walking into the house and simply saying, 'It's him,'" Perry said. "This is when I started to believe the unbelievable and this is the day my mother stopped marking the calendar with big Xs, which kept track of the days left of Lee's tour in Vietnam."

For Margaretta, who died in 1996, it was too much sadness, coming so soon after Ernest's death. "I don't think she ever recovered from my brother's death," said Dan. "She had other children to take care of, so she made an effort, but I don't think she ever regained her spirit."

"I don't know how my mom handled it as well as she did. She hurt deeply," Jean said. "My mom went through a lot of losses, but she always had a smile. I cannot imagine the heartbreak."

Dan had his own difficulties. "I don't think I dealt with it very well in the short term. I abused alcohol for several years. When you abuse alcohol, you don't go through the regular grief process," he said.

After treatment in 1979, Dan was able to put it in focus. Today, he says he has accepted it and moved on.

"As the years passed and the acceptance of Lee's death deepened, I would often wonder what had happened over there," Perry said. "How was he killed? Was it quick? Did he suffer? Did he cry for his mother? Was he alone? Was it friendly fire?"

"The hurt is always there," Jean said. "I think about my brother every day." She recalls talking to a niece about Lee for a school paper the girl was doing. Jean broke down and cried trying to talk about it.

Unexpected visit

The family has been mostly supportive of Purinton's pilgrimage. "I can only wonder how hard it was for Wayne to make that phone call (to us), not knowing how we would react. I know Wayne was very concerned about opening old wounds," Perry said.

Jean had mixed feelings about it, and asked her brothers to respond to Purinton.

"But I'm really glad he's doing this. I can't imagine what he's been through," Jean said. "It brings back some sad memories, but any thought process is a bit more intellectual than emotional," Dan said. "But if we as a family can help Wayne Purinton with his healing process—I think it's good that he's doing it."

Men in uniform brought tragic news to Cadott family

(Author's note: This is an editorial news article)

Jean Poehls was home alone when she saw the vehicle carrying two uniformed men pull into the driveway of her rural Cadott home in January 1968. "I looked out the window and said, 'Oh my God, no.'" She recalls.

For a family with a loved one in the American armed forces during war time, there can be no more dreaded sight than those uniformed men bringing news to the door.

In recent weeks, Jean and her brothers and sister have relived that moment when they heard the news of the death of their brother, Lee Danielson, in Vietnam, on Jan. 12, 1968. The man who was lying next to Lee when he was killed—a man still dealing with the trauma that war left on his soul—had called and wanted to talk about Lee, and visit his grave.

They did so this Memorial Day weekend. Lee Danielson's family is less in need of a reminder of the high price of war than most American citizens are this Memorial Day. The day honoring our war dead has become for some a sparsely attended ceremony, with faceless names read aloud and plastic wreaths placed by cold stone, all interrupting plans for that perfect cook-out.

But if you need a reminder of what this Memorial Day is really all about, listen to the Danielson's story: Those men in that car first stopped at the Cadott

Post Office to ask for directions to the home of Margaretta and the late Ernest Danielson. People knew what a visit from such men meant. "Cadott was a little like Mayberry, and it did not take long for news to spread through the town," said Perry Danielson, Lee's brother, who was 13 at the time. Perry and his mother had gone to Eau Claire to pick up some slides from films Lee had sent home.

Cadott's police officer, Margaretta's nephew, had been notified to keep an eye out for the family car. "When we were coming home, driving through Cadott, the Cadott cop stopped us and told my mother, 'Aunt Margaretta, I got a phone call and you are supposed to go home.' I think that my mother knew instantly and tears started to roll down her cheeks," Perry said.

She drove a block to a place called The Corner Store and called home. The family's minister answered. "She started to cry and handed the phone to me," Perry recalls. "The minister asked me where we were and in what seemed like only five minutes, the store's door opened and in walked our neighbor, minister and two men in uniform. So inside that little store is where my mother and I were officially notified of Lee's death."

Jean and her older sister, Sharon, already knew. When Jean saw those men in that car she kept telling herself that Lee was "hurt." With a sense of compassion to which we should all aspire, Jean felt sorry for the elderly man who led the duo delivering the bad news. He asked for her mother, and clearly did not want to tell this 17-year-old child about her brother's death.

Jean's only support nearby was a distant cousin, Harland Danielson, who was doing some work by the barn he rented from them.

Finally, Jean said to the uniformed gentleman, "He's hurt, right?" The man's eyes filled with tears. "I just went running to (Harland). I was just so thankful that he was there," Jean said.

The oldest of the family was Sharon, away at college at River Falls at the time. "Out of the clear blue sky Sharon called about 20 minutes later," Jean said. "I couldn't talk to her. They had to tell her over the phone."

Darrell, known as Dan, was the oldest boy in the family. He was in the Navy, stationed in Ireland. "I got the message from one of the troops there that the captain wanted to see me. I knew immediately what it was for," he said. "It was devastating for me. I was in a daze."

He was quickly flown back. All the way, in the common stage of grief known as "denial," he held to the hope of some sort of a military mix-up.

But he was at the airport in Eau Claire when the casket arrived. He and some uncles accompanied the casket to the funeral home in Cadott, where they had to identify the body. "I can still vividly remember Darrell coming back home and walking into the house and simply saying, 'It's him.' "This is when I started to believe the unbelievable and this is the day my mother stopped marking the calendar with big Xs, which kept track of the days left of Lee's tour in Vietnam," Perry said. Thus a family dealt with the reality of what we give cursory notice to in our ceremonies.

The victims of war are not just names etched on the stones. They were real people, loved by their families in the same way our own families love us. They were not the only victims of war that deserve to be honored on Memorial Day.

Look around at the ceremony Monday, and you will see flesh and blood victims of war. They are the people who saw men like Lee die, and to this day struggle with the vivid images haunting their lives. They are the family members like Jean Poehls who saw that car carrying uniformed men turn into the driveway. They are the brothers, sisters, uncles and aunts who got that fateful call.

To them, the lonesome sound of "Taps" does not just signal the end of a ceremony. It echoes in an empty place in their hearts.[12]

Ken Baldwin's account of that January 12, 1968 firefight

(Transcribed from taped interview)

"We were airlifted on top of a hill and there was a village down below. The story I got at the time was that we were put on the hill so we could rest a little bit, because we were really under strength. We were tired and worn out. We did not have a whole lot of people. Captain Davison had become our Company Commander not too long before that.

"After we set up a perimeter on that hill, he decided to send a patrol out. We were all kind of grouchy. You know we were supposed to set up a perimeter and be safe and rest for a little bit. We needed some time to recuperate. So he sent the 1st platoon down to the village on patrol, while the 3rd platoon finished digging in. The 3rd platoon was then supposed to go down the other side of the village and patrol.

"We hadn't left yet, but the 1st platoon was already down there when they really stepped into it. I was told it was an NVA headquarters company, anti-aircraft company, and support companies, so it was a pretty good size group.

"They 'stepped in it' and a firefight ensued. We were ordered to saddle up with light gear and go down the other side of the hill. There was a rice paddy between us. We just had a new lieutenant who came in to replace Lt. Beck. Lt. Beck had been promoted to Company Executive Officer.

"Our new lieutenant, Lt. Smith, ordered us to get down there in some low cover behind the rice paddy on our side. On the other side of the village was where the firefight was going on. Lt. Smith told us, (Stan Roden was the squad leader), 'Take your squad and go across.' That was the squad I was in and I was walking point, so I went first. So I took off. We were going across the rice paddy dike to the other side. I didn't know what was going on, but I'm looking behind me and running for all I'm worth to get across the rice paddy dike.

"I guess there was firing going on the other side. Stan and I were the only two who made it across. As I went across, I didn't stop. I started running up a trail. About five or ten feet from me, this bush starts shaking and smoking, and I'm going, 'Oh no!' I ran full tilt forward and planted a foot and jumped over a little hedgerow into a potato field or hills or rows. We called it a potato field, I don't know what it was, just a field that had rows in it.

"I'm lying down behind one of these rows and I hollered back, 'Don't go up the trail. There is a gun emplacement.' So Stan had stopped. He said 'Okay.' Of course, I was hunkered down behind this row as far as I could get and still get some fire. I told him to 'Fire on that.' I wanted to get back. He said, 'Okay.' What actually happened was I said, 'Okay, I'm coming back to your position.' "So I got up and looked. As I was running, I tripped, and I remember looking up and seeing this grenade, and I fell. I fell in between the rows, and, as I was falling down, I could look and see the grenade was coming down with me. So I went down, I put my rifle down and grabbed hold of my helmet and hunkered down. The grenade hit about a foot or so in front of me and went off. I was so close to it that it blew over me, but the concussion was so bad it had my head ringing, I couldn't hear anything. It felt like it just lifted me off the ground. Stan was hollering, 'Are you okay? You okay?' I was going, 'Yeah, well, as soon as I get the bells out of my head, I'll be alright.' Then I hollered at him, 'Give me some fire here. I'm pinned down.' So he opened up, and I waited about a six count, and then I stuck my rifle up over my head and fired a whole magazine. I put another magazine in and ran back to where Stan was lying.

"We were still on the other side of the rice paddy, and, as you went across the rice paddy dike, it went up again about three feet into a plowed field. It then went over a field down to that three-foot drop off before it went to the paddy Stan and I were in, and that's the first time I realized we were the only two who came across. I didn't know that fire was coming both ways. So Stan and I are standing there looking at each other thinking this is not a good place to be, especially with just the two of us. We decided to go back across the paddy where the rest of the platoon was located. Stan looked at me and I looked at him. I said, 'We got to get back.' He said, 'Yeah, we do.' On the count of one, two, we both took off running. We didn't get back on the dike, we ran through the paddy. Have you ever tried to run through knee-deep mud? We pretty much stayed on top of it. I remember finally getting across to the other side.

"I got back to the other side and sat down behind a big rock. I had taken my helmet off, and then incoming rounds started hitting again. I remember thinking, *Where's my helmet? I lost my helmet! I need my helmet!* It was sitting right between my legs. *Oh, there it is*, and I got it back on, and that's when I found out that Lee had been killed. I didn't go up and check, but I saw the medic was with him, and the medic just kind of looked at me, shook his head and said, 'There's not much I can do for him.' Come to find out that Lee had been directing cover fire for Stan and me with the M-60 machine gun, and that's when he was killed.

"We stayed in contact with the enemy until dusk. The 1st platoon was trapped over there on the other side of the village. They worked their way around and came across that rice paddy dike where we were located. I can remember seeing them coming over that drop-off, and, just as it got dusk, they infiltrated back as we gave them cover fire. We went back up the hill that night to the company perimeter as they (the company) were calling in artillery and gunships. When we started back up the hill, we wanted to make sure we brought everyone with us. We didn't want to leave anyone, especially one of our own.

"I helped carry Lee part way back up the hill. Then somebody took my place and I went to the back to provide cover in case the NVA were on our trail. When we got back to the top of the hill, I remember telling the first sergeant that

Lee had been killed.

"We stayed on the perimeter that night, and the next morning we went back down to go through the village. There were very few guys from the 1st platoon that weren't wounded still with us. I remember that morning I heard a shot. One of the guys in the 1st platoon shot himself in the foot, so that he wouldn't have to go back down there. After what he had been through the night before, he said, 'I can't go back down there.' He was ordered, 'Well, we are going back down there.' He said, 'I can't go.' And that's when he shot himself.

"I remember going back down there and sweeping through the village and seeing that gun emplacement where I was running up the trail. They found the gun that was shooting at me. There was a gun in the hole and a lot of blood, but there weren't any bodies left in the area.

Come to find out, that trail that I had run up, we had apparently taken out that gun position. It was the same trail that the 1st platoon was able to escape on, because we had made a hole in the perimeter of the ambush and they were able to escape."

Medal of Honor Recipient

William D. Port was a member of the 1st platoon. That was the platoon we were sent down to help out when they were pinned down by enemy fire. Port joined the Army from Harrisburg, Pennsylvania, and by January 12, 1968, was serving as a private first class in Company C, 5th Battalion, 7th Cavalry Regiment, 1st Air Cavalry Division.

During a firefight on that day, in the Que Son Valley, Quang Nam Province, Republic of Vietnam, Port rescued a wounded comrade and then smothered the blast of an enemy-thrown grenade with his body to protect other soldiers. Port survived the blast but was seriously wounded and captured by the enemy. He died while a prisoner of war ten months later. Port was promoted to sergeant and posthumously awarded the Medal of Honor for his actions during the battle.

Port, aged twenty-seven at his death, was buried in Arlington National Cemetery, Arlington County, Virginia. In Huntingdon, Pennsylvania, there is a bridge across the Juniata River named after William Port. A plaque describes his heroism.

Quote from Steve Loving[13], a member of the 1st platoon: "Bill was drafted at a much older age than most of us kids—we were mostly eighteen or nineteen and even the officers were in their early twenties. Bill was in his late twenties. While most of us always seemed to have something to gripe about, I can never recall Bill saying anything negative. He was a quiet, private guy and he led his life that way—with quiet dignity. That dreadful day in January is a day that our platoon will never forget, and many of us are able to celebrate life because of Bill's sacrifice. He will never be forgotten by any of us who served with him."

Citation: For conspicuous gallantry and intrepidity at the risk of his own life above and beyond the call of duty. Sgt. Port distinguished himself while serving as a rifleman with Company C, which was conducting combat operations against an enemy force in the Que Son Valley. As Sgt. Port's platoon was moving to cut off a reported movement of enemy soldiers, the platoon came under heavy fire from an entrenched enemy force. The platoon was forced to withdraw due to the intensity and ferocity of the fire. Although wounded in the hand as the withdrawal began, Sgt. Port, with complete disregard for his safety, ran through the heavy fire to assist a wounded comrade to the safety of the platoon perimeter. As the enemy forces assaulted the perimeter, Sgt. Port and three comrades were in position behind an embankment when an enemy grenade landed in their midst. Sgt. Port, realizing the danger to his fellow soldiers, shouted the warning, "Grenade," and unhesitatingly hurled himself toward the grenade to shield his comrades from the explosion. Through his exemplary courage and devotion he saved the lives of his fellow soldiers and gave the members of his platoon the inspiration needed to hold their position. Sgt. Port's selfless concern for his comrades, at the risk of his life above and beyond the call of duty are in keeping with the highest tradition of the military service and reflect great credit on himself, his unit, and the U.S. Army.[14]

William D. Port Photo Courtesy of Steve Loving

12 Jan 68

1055 hr 1ˢᵗ lift of Co C off PZ Colt at 1010H to LZ BT015376 at 1015 SITREP Green. Lift complete at 1045H.

1355 hr Co C 2/8 ele vic 021363 spotted 2 M/A males evading, negative weapons, reconned with mortars.

1415 hr Co C at BT013364 received 1 Sniper rnd from the West and will recon by mortars.

1429 hr Co C request MED EVAC for WIA's from sniper fire at BT014365. They are receiving sniper fire & frags.

1646 hr Co C request MED EVAC for the 1/6 at loc BT017360 complete.

1856 hr 5/7 Command Chopper is needed to up to pick up the 5/7 CO and drop off resupply at Co C loc.

1904 hr Co C **2/6 ele has linked up with 1/6 ele and is trying to recover the**

WIA's & KIA's at this time.

1915 hr Co C <u>ele are trying to get back to CP location at this time. They have the 1/6 ele & wounded also.</u> Will wait until they reach CP to bring in MEDEVAC. The count is 10 or 12 WIA's & 2 KIA's.

1930 hr Co C request MED EVAC for Co C at vic BT015375. MED EVAC complete.

2010 hr Co C MED EVAC complete for 4 WIA & 1 KIA on the 1st MED EVAC at 2010H. The 2nd MED EVAC complete at 2030 H for 6 WIA's.

SUMMARY

Co C at 1055H conducted an air move to vic BT0153876 and relieved Co D of the mission of securing the high ground. At 1429H 2 plts of Co C began to receive sniper fire in the vic of BT014365. **The contact developed and the 2 elements were pinned down by an enemy force estimated to be 1 NVA company. One platoon became partially surrounded and cut off.** Two plts of Co A were inserted into the contact area and successfully assisted in breaking contact and the withdrawal of all elements. Contact continued until approximately 1930H at which time the element were able to withdraw to their Co's loc. The results of the action were 1 US KIA, 3 US MIA, 11 WIAs enemy casualties are not available at this time.

CHAPTER EIGHTEEN

Moving Base Camp

January 18, 1968

Dear Mom and Dad,

Hi. I have some time this evening, so will write you a few lines. I received your letter yesterday. Sure glad to hear from you. Why did you ask if I had hocked my cameras? No, I haven't. I have about $50 wrapped up in them. I have been carrying the 16mm out here in the field and the other two are locked up in An Khe. The Polaroid would be a good camera to use at home, as it takes color prints in 60 seconds. I am down to 68 days left in the field. Write soon.

Your son,

Wayne

January 22, 1968

Dear Mom and Dad,

Hi. I received a letter from you today, so will try and get a letter written this eve-
ning. I was sure glad to hear from you. The 1ˢᵗ Cavalry Division is moving base
camp from An Khe up to Hue, which is north of Danang, so will be close to the
DMZ and Marines. I heard that Chuck may be going in the Army soon. Sure
hope he decides to enlist, because he sure doesn't want to be out here. This has
been a long hard year and sure will be glad when it's over with, but think I have
learned a lot from it. A battle is something most people read about or watch on
TV. I will never forget January 12ᵗʰ, as we really got in a fix. We were caught in
the open while enemy machine gun fire raked the ground. It was really a shock
to see my buddy lying there with a hole in his head. I am doing pretty good, but
am kind of rundown and have a cold. It is about dark, so will close for now. Hope
everyone is fine and write soon. Will pay the phone bill when I get home, as I
cannot draw any money out now.

Lots of love

Your son,

Wayne

January 22, 1968

Dear Eddie,

Hi! How's everything with you? This will be kind of short as it is nearly dark. We
have to go on an ambush at 5 O'clock in the morning. Sure hate those things.
The 25ᵗʰ of January, we are going up to Hue to set up a new base camp. That is
only a few miles from the DMZ. How are you doing in basketball? Do you still
have that old car? Have you been doing any hunting? Well, can hardly see, so
will close. Write.

Wayne

January 22, 1968

Dear Ron,

Hi. Just a few lines this evening as it is about dark. The Cavalry is moving in a couple of days to Hue by the DMZ. How have you been making out with that girl lately? How did you do on the tests? How do you like college by now? I sure am tired of this place and only have 69 days left. I just hope we don't get in anymore fire fights like January 12th, as I nearly got it then. The NVA opened up with a machine gun and I got caught in the open. I sure was kissing the ground. One of my buddies was killed right beside me. Guess I will close for now.

Wayne

January 24, 1968

Dear Eddie,

Guess I will write you a few lines to wish you a HAPPY BIRTHDAY. Not much is new with me. We are still waiting to move up to Hue (pronounced like the word "way") probably tomorrow or the next day. We got a bunch of new guys in the company today. Sure glad to see them come as we are short of men. So many of our guys are sick or wounded. Well, I cannot think of much else, so will close for now. HAPPY BIRTHDAY!

Wayne

January 31, 1968

Dear Mom and Dad,

Hi. Sorry I haven't written sooner, but have been busy lately. We landed in Quang Tri on the 26th and the first night there, had 140 mm rockets come in on us. The battalion CO was killed along with some other guys. The next day, by truck convoy we moved south to a Marine base between Quang Tri and Hue along Highway 1. Did you ever get that map I sent? How's the weather? It's been hot here. I have 58 days after tomorrow here. Sure will be glad to leave here. Guess this will be all for now.

Lots of love,

Wayne

CHAPTER NINETEEN

Tet Offensive 1968

The division began 1968, by terminating Operation Pershing, the longest of the 1st Cavalry's Vietnam actions. When the operation ended on 21 January, the enemy had lost 5,401 soldiers and 2,400 enemy soldiers had been captured. In addition, some 1,300 individual and 137 crew weapons had been captured or destroyed.

Moving to I Corps, Vietnam's northernmost tactical zone, the division set up Camp Evans for their base camp. On January 31, 1968, amid the celebration of the Vietnamese New Year, the enemy launched the Tet Offensive, a major effort to overrun South Vietnam. Some 7,000 enemy, well-equipped, crack NVA regulars blasted their way into the imperial city of Hue, overpowering all but a few pockets of resistance held by ARVN troops and the U.S. Marines. Within twenty-four hours, the invaders were joined by 7,000 NVA reinforcements. Almost simultaneously to the North of Hue, five battalions of North Vietnamese and Viet Cong attacked Quang Tri City, the capital of Vietnam's Northern Province.

Following fierce fighting at Thon La Chu, the 3rd Brigade moved toward the embattled city of Hue. The southwest wall of the city was soon taken after 1st Battalion, 7th Cavalry overcame severe resistance and linked up the 5th Battalion, 7th Cavalry. At this point, the NVA and Viet Cong invaders were driven from Hue by late February. The Tet Offensive was over. The NVA and Viet Cong had suffered a massive defeat, with 32,000 killed and 5,800 captured.[3]

February 9, 1968

Dear Mom and Dad,

Hi. I know I have not written in a long time, <u>but we have been under constant mortar attacks this month.</u> I have been living in a fox hole for days now; sure do hope things let up for awhile. How's everybody back there? I hope ok. I have 51 days to go yet, but some of the guys leaving now are getting 5 to 15 day drops, so maybe I will too. I should be able to leave the field by March 20th for sure. Still would like to have you meet me in Denver, and if I can find the car I want, will try and get it. I am thinking about a Dodge Cornett. Well, really cannot think of much more, so will close. Hope this finds everyone ok.

Lots of love,

Wayne

During the Vietnam War, soldiers received many letters of support, a lot of them from high school girls. Here is one such letter that I received.

February 9, 1968

Dear Soldier,

I'm a student at Lincoln Senior High School and our English class decided to write to the men in Vietnam. It's hard to realize that all the fighting I read about is actually happening. It doesn't become a reality until someone close goes. No one in my family is in Vietnam, but my brother's friends are. I hope the war can end as soon as possible, but while it lasts, remember I'm behind you 100%. I hope you will answer and tell me about how you live and what it is like.

Sincerely,

Donna Hulme

9 Feb 68

0835 hr <u>**3 incoming mortar rds.**</u> Co C has 4 WIA, req MED EVAC

0845 hr <u>**more incoming mortar rds.**</u>

0845 hr Co C has 5 Ln 2's, Ln # 56, 137, not MED EVACED Ln # 216, 242, 226 MED EVACED on log bird.

0900 hr Co C has more wounded, req MED EVAC. In # 59, 220, 222, 242, 216, 226, 137, 204. Tail # 455 Complete 0935H.

0930 hr C Co spotted indiv evading to their front, took under fire.

0937 hr Co C had <u>**1 more incoming mortar rd,**</u> req MED EVAC for Ln # 156.

0952 hr Co C # 156 was MED EVAC on log bird.

1345 hr C Co <u>**received mortars,**</u> req MED EVAC for Ln # 6, 17, 51, 116, 134, & Sr Medic. Ln #101, 219, 100, 148 were not MED EVACED.

1418 hr Co C MEDEVAC complete, chopper was fired at by M79 on approach.

1427 hr C Co <u>**still receiving sporadic mortar fire.**</u>

SUMMARY

Co C at 0835H vic YD683255 <u>**received sporadic mortar fire**</u> lasting approx 2 hours and resulting in 19 WIA. At 0930H, same loc, spotted unk nr of indiv evading to their front, engaged with neg assessment.

February 10, 1968

Dear Mom and Dad,

Hi! Just a few lines this evening to let you know I am ok. Received your letters today and was glad to hear as we have not gotten any mail in over a week. Things were a little better today, as only 10 mortar rounds came in. We are just a few miles NW of Hue. We were supposed to go there, but have been making contact here, guess the Marines are about to get Hue back. All the money I make over here is tax free and will bring it home in government checks. I am really looking forward to getting a car when I get back. I was glad to get the VFW card. I have decided not to smoke, as I know I might regret it in later years and really can't get much out of it anyway. I do smoke a pipe once in awhile in the evening. Well, really cannot think of much more, so will close.

Lots of love,

Wayne

February 12, 1968

Dear Wayne,

Guess it is time that I write you another letter. It might not be as long as the last one, but at least I will be writing a few lines. Today is Lincoln's birthday. I can't believe that almost a whole year has gone by since we last saw each other. It seems like a short time has gone by. I'm getting anxious to see you. I don't know if you're too anxious to get home, but I know I will be glad to see you. Today, we had a small program in school. Last November the whole student body pitched in their entire penny's they could spare and bought a plaque honoring the boys (men) from TCHS fighting in the war in Viet Nam. I thought of you the whole time. I guess no one here at home really knows what it is like over there. The ones that have been there and returned don't want to talk about it. Guess from some of the things some of the boys have said about it, I would want to forget too. You never seem to write much about it. I guess you don't want to. There really isn't much else for you to write about though, is there? I guess it is true when they say war changes you. I can tell a lot of difference between the letters I received from you in Denver and the ones I get now. There is just a slight change, but there it is. I've been changing too. Day after tomorrow is Valentine's Day. Happy Valentine's Day!! Guess that isn't much, but it will have to do. I'll send you a card later. Ok?! Graduation is steadily drawing nearer. I'm getting all excited and restless. It seems like it will never get here. I guess after it does, I'll wish it wouldn't have. I bet you would like to be back in dear TCHS. HA!! How long are you going to be home? I hope for quite a while. I hope you will see me when you come home. I want to see you. Take care, write soon and I miss you.

Love you,

Dianne

P.S. We're all thinking of you back here. All my friends and yours say HI and hurry home!

Reflections

Reflecting back today on Dianne's letter dated February 12, 1968, I can understand that no one at home really knew what it was like in Vietnam. Dianne wrote, "You never seem to write much about it. I guess you don't want to. There really isn't much else for you to write about though, is there?"

While on patrol in the dense jungles or rice paddies, I had to be on constant alert for the enemy. During a lull in the action, whether sitting in a rice paddy or jungle trail taking a break, or in my hooch at night, writing Dianne and others was a way for me to temporarily escape the insanity of the war. I didn't have to think about the circumstances that had led me to where I was in life that day. I was there, all I could do was try to deal with it. For those few minutes, I could daydream of better days to come. Writing home grim details about my combat experiences would have made her upset and worry about my safety. I was trying to shield her from the reality of combat.

Vietnam must have seemed somewhat like a mysterious place to those at home who could only try to imagine what it was like over there. Most of the guys coming home didn't want to talk about it, which I believe, in turn, led people at home to wonder even more about the war. What was really happening over there that no one wanted to talk about when they came back to the World? Once home, I didn't want to think about the war. I just wanted to move on with my life and bury my wartime experiences. Combat is a life-changing experience and, as Dianne said in her letter, "I guess it is true when they say war changes you."

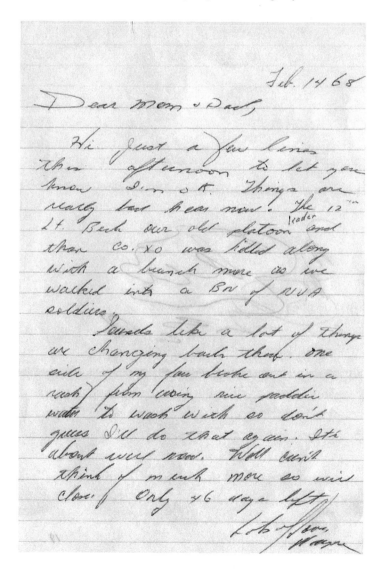

12 Feb 68

1255 hr Co C fd fresh blood in their Obj area loc YD 682248.

1320 hr Co C receiving sniper rds YD 682248.

1755 hr Co C has 2 Ln # 2's condition not known.

1950 hr All 5-7 ele still trying to get all WIA's out, MED EVAC has been requested. Have 5 WIA's in pick-up posture, ARA & gunships still on station.

2027 hr Co C has 2 NVA KIA, 1 AK-47, all wounded out for Co C; all wounded out for Co A, still trying to get to two KIA's (friendly).

SUMMARY

Co C attacked on the right flank objective with negative resistance. At 1800H they followed Co A to protect their right flank and received an enemy counter attack from that flank resulting in 2 KIA & 8 WIA. They killed 5 NVA (bc) and estimated an additional 5.

Lieutenant Winfield Beck's Death

I have very few memories of the day that Lt. Beck was killed. What I do remember is lying flat on the ground, crawling as fast as I could, back toward our company as AK-47 bullets cracked overhead from one direction and M-16 bullets flew from the other direction. We were near the village of Thon La Chu and had walked right into a well-entrenched company of NVA soldiers. We had been caught in a crossfire with no place to go.

I was scared out of my wits. I continued trying to crawl to a safer place. I remember that I finally was able to find my way back to our side and find some cover. The next thing I remember is that mortar rounds started coming in on our position. One round hit so close to one of our guys that he went flying and screaming in pain through the air. I don't remember if he survived. There didn't seem to be any place to go that was safe. The mortar rounds continued to fall for a short time, and I was wondering if the next one would hit me. We eventually were able to retreat away from the village, taking our dead and wounded with us.

February 14, 1968

Dear Wayne,

Just a few minutes to spare before I get ready to go to bed. I studied English for about an hour and half. I really get so sick of studying all the time, but can never get anywhere if I don't. Practice for the **Sound Of Music** *is coming along just fine. I can't believe all the Latin I have to learn. It really is a lot of fun though. I can't wait till we put it on for the public. It should really be different. I don't quite know how we are going to do it, but I guess there's a way for everything. How are things with you? There really isn't much I can ask you. I just write about what I've been doing and the dumb things that are going on around school. It seems that even though we have known each other for a little over four years, I still find it hard to write you. I really don't know why, but I do find it hard. Ron and I talk quite a lot. Every so often, we'll ride around together on Saturday afternoons. He seems to really like going to school in Colby. I guess it is pretty different from Hays. He has a real nice car. I've been trying to talk Mom and Dad into buying me a car, but it just doesn't seem to work. I'll live without one. I don't know if I will get the newest model or if I'll get one a few years younger. Well, guess it is rolling around to my bedtime. Take care and write soon!*

Love ya,

Dianne

February 16, 1968

Dear Mom, Dad and Ed,

Guess I will try and write you a few lines this evening. That rash I had turned out to be ringworm and am having a hard time getting rid of it, but am supposed to get some stuff tomorrow for it. How's everybody there? Do you think you can work it so you can meet me in Denver, as it's only 42 days until I come home? Is Chuck joining the Army for sure? What kind of school does he want? Sure would hate to see him end up here. Write soon!

Lots of love, Wayne

February 19, 1968

Dear Mom, Dad and Ed,

Thought I would write you a few lines this afternoon. I am doing ok. Hope every-one is doing fine. We have been sitting in this village now for about 10 days. There is not much new with me. I received candy from Aunt Ruby and card from Aunt Mae. I am hoping your package will come in the mail today, as I am really hungry. One of the guys in our squad was wounded today while we were on patrol. <u>We ran into VC snipers shooting from trees.</u> Guess this will be all. Write soon.

Lots of love,

Wayne

19 Feb 68
1030 hr Co C <u>**received 5-6 rds sniper fire from tree line**</u> vic 683276, Arty cranking.
1130 hr Co C spt 2 indivs w/blk PJs, eng w/neg assessment, vic 684275.
1140 hr Co C spt 2 possible 3 indiv at 680276, eng w/SA neg assessment.

SUMMARY

Co C at 1030H <u>**received 5-6 sniper rds from vic 683276,**</u> eng w/arty, neg assessment. At 1130H spotted 2 indivs with blk PJs at 684275, eng w/SA, neg assessment. At 1140H spt 2-3 indiv at 680276, eng w/SA w/neg assessment.

February 19, 1968

Hi Eddie,

I have a few more minutes to write before I have to go out on a LP, so thought I would write you a letter. How's school coming along for you this New Year? How's the basketball team doing? I still have 41 days left here and sure am anx-

ious to come back there. Sure am hoping I can get a car. You realize I haven't driven anything for about a year now, so will seem kind of funny at first. Well, guess I better close for now. Write!

Love,

Wayne

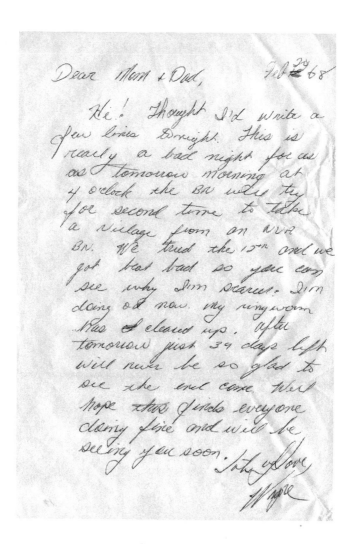

Remembering Zygmunt Paul Jablonski Jr.

On February 21, following fierce fighting that day in Thon Que Chu and

Thon La Chu, small villages northwest of Hue, the 5th Battalion, 7th Cavalry set up a perimeter of defense before light gave way to darkness. We were ordered by the platoon sergeant to dig in and prepare in case the NVA attacked our position during the night. It had been a long day of fighting, and I was tired and worn out. I recall some hot chow was flown in to us from Camp Evans.

I remember Ken Baldwin was picked first for guard duty that evening. My shift would come later in the night. A moderately strong northeast monsoon rain had moved into the area on February 1, and on the 21, the weather continued to hamper our operations against the NVA and the Viet Cong, as it favored their strategy. Heavy ground fog was particularly dense at night, and only diminished slightly during the day. The temperatures were a bone chilling 10 degrees below the expected minimum, between 40 and 50 degrees, making it even more miserable.

Ken had just gotten off guard duty and was getting comfortable in his hooch when the explosions started. He hadn't bothered to take his boots off, he just wanted to get some rest. I was sleeping soundly in my hooch when I was suddenly startled awake by the noisy outburst. At first, I couldn't figure out what was happening. Then, all of a sudden, another round came whistling in near our position, sending shrapnel flying in all directions. It was pitch dark, so it was difficult to tell what was going on. Were we under attack or was it just a couple of stray mortar rounds dropped in by the NVA?

I learned later that just as the second round came in, Zygmunt Jablonski, a member of our squad, was sitting up in his hooch, either taking his boots off or putting them on, no one knew for sure. He was hit in the chest and died from multiple fragmentation wounds. I heard someone call for a medic. I walked up near where he was lying, and even though the night was dark, I remember his face was ashen white. We stayed on alert the rest of the night. The next morning, I noticed my own hooch was full of shrapnel holes. I often wondered if I was plain lucky, or a divine presence saved me from harm that night.

Zygmunt Paul Jablonski Jr. of Chicopee Falls, Massachusetts, was born 6 June, 1947. He died 21 February, 1968 in Thua Thien Province, South Vietnam, at the age of twenty, attaining the rank of Private First Class (E-3). His name is inscribed on the Vietnam Veterans Memorial in Washington DC on the east wall, panel 40, line 53.

On reflection, I can remember being numb to the whole thing. It was only a few weeks earlier, January 12, that Sgt. Lee Danielson had been killed right before my eyes. Just eight days before, February 13, Lt. Winfield Beck had died in this same war-torn village. Jablonski's death seemed to hit me harder, as I only had a few days to go until I could leave the field and the war behind. I recall never being so glad to see the end come to this nightmare I was living.

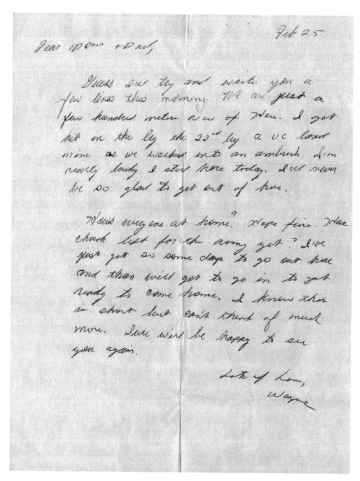

NVA Roadblock

On February 22, the final push to Hue began. Shortly before we reached a tree line one-half mile north of Hue along Highway 1, Lt. Michael Smith's third platoon, the one I was in, rotated from the lead and another platoon took point. As we started moving again, I was walking flank on the east side of the highway, about twenty yards out in a rice paddy field. The rice paddy was mucky from all the rain that had fallen during the month of February. We hadn't had a chance to shower or change clothes in weeks. I was tried and beaten down by over twenty days of fighting. As always, I didn't know what to expect as we approached Hue, but from all that had happened so far that month, I was very nervous and scared.

As we continued south along Highway 1, just a half-mile short of the city walls, a cleverly concealed NVA roadblock shattered the lead squad and engaged our company in locked combat. Our company came under heavy fire from an estimated company-size force of North Vietnamese, who occupied the hamlet of Thon An, approximately one kilometer from the An Hoa Bridge. When the snipers hit us, the NVA had the place honeycombed with bunkers, recoilless rifles, mortars, AK-47s, and machine guns. It was a well-defended roadblock. I like to call it an ambush, although our Company Commander, Captain Michael S. Davison Jr., didn't like that term. He preferred to call it a "roadblock."

I vividly remember walking along in the rice paddy that morning when all of a sudden, landmines began to detonate all around me. It scared the hell out of me! I began to retreat back toward the CP (command post). As I was running, trying to get out of the minefield, one exploded near my right and I felt hot shrapnel hit my leg. I must have thought I was wounded badly, as I began to call for a medic. In reality, the shrapnel had penetrated my pant leg and I had suffered a surface wound. I remember thinking that I made it almost a year in the field without being wounded or killed by the enemy, just to have this wound inflicted on me. I was extremely lucky I hadn't been injured more seriously during this combat incident.

After the initial surprise by the NVA, our company pulled back along Highway 1. Lieutenant Colonel James B. Vaught, Commander of the 5th Battalion, 7th Cavalry, called for Cobra helicopter gunships and artillery to attack the tree line. As I recall, the supporting fire continued throughout the day, but the Communist troops did not abandon their positions. With darkness approaching, Lt. Col. Vaught decided to call off the attack until the next morning.

That night, we dug in and cleared and checked our fields of fire. In the meantime, U.S. artillery continued to pound the hamlet of Thon An until the next morning. I had survived one more day of this hell. I didn't know what tomorrow would bring, but hopefully this would soon come to an end.

The next day, the battalion fought past the roadblock, and on February 25, we reached Hue's outer wall, where we hooked up with the 1st Battalion, 7th Cavalry, and the battle for Hue ended.

22 Feb 68

0830 hr Co C has fd 1 NVA gas mask, 1 medical kit, 1 mortar sight, bipod for 60mm mortar, 2 Chicom grenades, while searching bunkers in contact area.

1025 hr Civilians told Co C that there was a NVA Co camped in their objective area.

1525 hr Req MED EVAC for Co C, Tail #298, Complete.

1620 hr ARA on station.

1705 hr Gunship report having rockets fired at him.

1720 hr 1 log bird full of detainees inbound to LZ Evans, nr unk.

1754 hr 1 log bird has just left w/10M/A males, 1 is confirmed VC or NVA.

1810 hr Co C WIA: 204, 130, 135, 90, not evaced: 124, 127 & 3 MIA.

1953 hr Co C Ln# 127 was not WIA.

2010 hr Items left in contact area today, 1 PRC 25 radio, 6 M-16.

SUMMARY

Co C moved with Bn to contact area where the Co sustained 8 WIA and 1 MIA, from well entrenched snipers and mortars from an unknown location. Lost 1 PCR 25, and 6 M-16 in contact area.

February 25, 1968

Dear Mom, Dad and Ed,

Well, guess I will write you a few lines this evening. I received a letter from Grandma, Dianne and some magazines from Aunt Ruby. I still have not gotten the package yet, but guess the mail is slow now. Things have quieted down some now. They have Hue under control. We are just on the edge of it now. Well, I cannot think of much more, so will close. Hope to hear from you soon.

Lots of love,

Wayne

February 26, 1968

Dear Mom and Dad,

Today, we got to go into Hue and look around as they have the city back now. The place sure is a mess, dead people all over the streets. I only got two pictures, as that's all of the film I had left. Tomorrow, we are going north a ways and work the area there. Hope to get my orders soon. Most of the guys are getting stationed at Ft Campbell, Ky, so might end up there or Ft Hood, Tx. They are also getting to come home 4 days early, so hope to get that. Well, hope this finds everyone ok.

Lots of love,

Wayne

February 26, 1968

Dear Wayne,

Well, I finally got a couple of letters from you. It was really great hearing from you. Boy, from the sound of your letter, you have really had your fill of Vietnam and the Army. Not but a few months ago, you were saying something about signing up to go back to Saigon for six more months. I really thought it was dumb, but I can't tell you what to do. You're your own boss and can make up your own mind. I saw your mom downtown and talked to her for a while. I told her I got a couple of letters from you. She was glad I heard from you. I'm happier than she is.

Love you,

Dianne

February 28, 1968

Dear Mom, Dad and Ed,

Guess I will write you a few lines this evening. How's everyone at home? I am doing just fine, am really tired. We have not had a chance to shower or change clothes since January. Saw in the paper where Bryce is in the Army. Has Chuck gone in yet? Our mail sure is slow. I still have not received that package you sent me. Only 20 days left out here. Do you think you can meet me in Denver? Anywhere from March 27th to April 1st. I will call you when I get there. Well, really cannot think of much more, so will close.

Lots of love,

Wayne

March 2, 1968

Dear Mom, Dad and Ed,

Hi! Just a few lines this morning to let you know I am doing ok. We were supposed to be air lifted to Camp Evans this morning, but has been raining all morning, so we may not get to go. How's everyone back there? Sure hope fine. Well, this is the month that I get to come home. I can hardly wait as I am really tired of this place. Seems like it has really been a long year. Hope this finds everyone ok.

Lots of love,

Wayne

March 4, 1968

Dear Mom, Dad and All,

Guess I will write a few lines this evening to let you know I am doing ok. Hope everyone there is too. We are going to stay at Camp Evans for two weeks, so when the Company goes back to the field, I will probably go on back to An Khe to get ready to come home. I have not been feeling very well lately, guess I am sort of run down. Guess this will be all for this time.

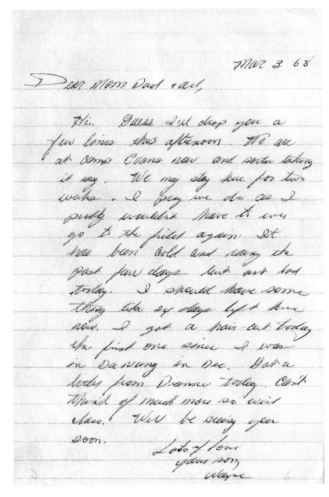

Lots of love,

Wayne

March 6, 1968

Dear Mom, Dad and All,

Hi. Received a letter from you today, so guess I will write a few lines this evening. How is everyone there? I am doing fine now. It is really nice here the past few days, the weather that is. Do you still think that you can come out to Denver, as I want to get a car for sure? Be sure and do not forget to bring my driver's license with you, as I haven't got one. I have been receiving mail from girls in Topeka, one from Delia, wonder where that is? Well, guess I will close for now. Will be seeing you soon.

Lots of love,

Wayne

March 8, 1968

Dear Folks,

Just a few lines this evening along with the film. I don't know how the pictures will turn out. I took them with Minolta 17. The last two were taken of the fight at Hue. How's everyone there? I have around 19 days left now. Guess it will not be too long until I get home. Is Chuck in the Army now? If you want to, just write one more letter when you get this. I will call when I get to Denver, which should be anytime from March 27 to April 1. Guess this is all for now.

Lots of love,

Wayne

February 28, 1968

Hi Guy!

I just thought I'd send you a real neat letter for once. I'm writing it on heavy paper and making it real big so you will surely be able to read it. Hey, since when have you become a TV star? Looks like you are really hitting it big. I've seen you on TV twice. Your Mom said she saw you a couple of weeks ago and then last night you were on the news again. Next time wave and give me a big smile. HA!! Nothing much has happened since yesterday when I wrote you. The school is really getting a good going-over. They have painted the restrooms, waxed the floors, washed the walls, and even cleaned the bricks on the outside of the building. They are really crazy. We are having some kind of evaluation this week and a bunch of people are going to be here looking over the school and asking a bunch of questions. Can't wait till they ask me what I think of the school. I'll tell them the truth. You know that picture you sent me from Manila? I finally got a real pretty frame for it. It is a white frame and really makes the picture look great. Of course, it looks great without the frame. Time is really beginning to pass. I'm so anxious for you to get home. We have a lot to talk over. Lots! It seems like a year has just been torn out of our lives and will never come back. When you get home we'll make up for all that lost time. Who knows we may go "dutch" all the time. Well, enough of my sentiment. Guess I'll just have to wait until you get home to see what happens. Maybe we've both changed to where we can't get along. It's a possibility. I sure hope not. I'm sending you a couple pieces of gum to give you lots of energy. Take care and write soon.

I love you,

Dianne

CBS Evening News Report

As the Tet Offensive continued into late February, the anchorman for the *CBS Evening News*, Walter Cronkite, traveled to Vietnam and filed several field reports. I don't recall the exact date, but I believe it was February 22 or 23, around the time of the NVA roadblock incident along Highway 1, a CBS news crew showed up to film us for the news. That encounter with CBS news accounted for my being seen by Dianne on TV during the evening news broadcast a day or two later.

Upon his return to the United States, Cronkite took an unprecedented step by presenting his editorial opinion at the end of the news broadcast on February 27. "For it seems now more certain than ever," Cronkite said, "that the bloody experience of Vietnam is to end in a stalemate." After watching the Cronkite broadcast, President Lyndon B. Johnson was quoted as saying, "That's it. If I've lost Cronkite, I've lost middle America."

March 9, 1968

Dear Mom and Dad,

Hi. Received your letter today and was sure glad to hear from you. Also, I received letters from Chuck, Aunt Luella and Dianne. Today, we went on a security mission down towards Hue on trucks. Dianne said she has seen me twice on TV. I sure must have looked a mess. Sure wish it would be so I wouldn't miss seeing Chuck, but guess by now he is in training. Well, sure hope this finds everyone ok. Will be seeing you soon.

Lots of love,

Wayne

March 9, 1968

Dear Wayne,

I'm adding a little color to your life. Just had a fantastic artistic urge and came up with this little rose. I would send you a dozen roses, but I can't afford it. Ha! **The Sound of Music** *went real well. Thursday night we had all but six rows in the back filled and Friday night every seat was filled. It was great to see so many people there. It was really great. Friday night at the end of the show every person stood for the cast. I guess it had to be pretty good or they wouldn't have stood. It makes all the time and effort we put into it all worthwhile. It was really sad Friday night. All the girls were crying. I was the biggest baby of all. I went down and bought this little card to give you a laugh. It isn't the greatest, but at least it is something different. I guess it will serve its purpose. I'm really confused about when you are coming home. I get some letters that say thirty, twenty, or more. Guess I'll just wait for a call or something. I guess you are still going to call me. Well, I have a test and report for tomorrow so I'd better get busy.*

Love ya,

Dianne

March 10, 1968

Dear Mom and Dad,

Just a few lines this evening to let you know I am doing ok. Guess what? Tonight, the company Commander asked me to be his radio operator, so guess I will have it made until I leave here. Tomorrow, we are making an air assault 10 miles south of here to set up a new firebase. Building bunkers and setting up a defense. I am ordering a 1ˢᵗ Cavalry ring, which is real pretty. It should be there at home by the middle of next month. Well, I sure am looking forward to coming home.

Lots of love,

Wayne

March 13, 1968

Dear Mom and Dad,

Hi. Guess I will start a letter now, but will probably have to finish this later on. How's everyone there? Received a letter from Grandma this morning. I still have not received the package from you. Well, by the time you get this letter, I should be on my way back down to An Khe and getting ready to come back to the States. We are making a new firebase today. It is warm, but rainy. I will write more later on and let you know where I am.

Lots of love,

Wayne

March 19, 1968

Dear Mom and Dad,

Hi. Just a few lines this morning. I haven't been too well lately and this morning found out I have some kind of worms. I am at Camp Evans and will be here until the 22ⁿᵈ, then may have to go back to the field, but will be going to An Khe the 27ᵗʰ, so if I do have to go back out in the field, I won't have much time left. It's not for sure, but don't expect me to call until somewhere around the 1ˢᵗ of April. I have just 12 days left here now. I sure am looking forward to getting back there. I took two shots this morning and have two more to take next week, and then all my shots will be up to date. Sure is hot here now. Will be seeing you real soon.

Lots of love,

Your son

Wayne

Ken Baldwin, left and author at Camp Evans. Photo Courtesy of Ken Baldwin

CHAPTER TWENTY

The Aftermath of War

I arrived back in the States in early April 1968. We flew into McChord Air Force Base, near Fort Lewis, Washington, on a cool rainy spring day. As we touched down on the tarmac, I gave a sigh of relief; I was safely back home, back in the World. The next day, after processing through Fort Lewis, I flew to Denver and had a surprise awaiting me at Stapleton International Airport. My aunt and uncle, Ruby and Elmer Cue had driven to the airport from their home near Arriba, Colorado, to greet me and welcome me home. It sure was a great feeling seeing familiar faces for the first time in over a year.

The very first thing I wanted to do when I arrived in Denver was go look at new cars. Dreaming about getting a new car when I returned home from my tour of duty had helped sustain me through some rough times. We drove to downtown Denver and I was able to look at some new cars, excited and happy that it wouldn't be long until I could drive one away from a car dealer's lot. My aunt and uncle then took me back to the airport to catch a flight back to Hays, Kansas.

When I arrived at the Hays airport, Mom, Dad, and two of my brothers were there to greet me. I was so happy to see my family and be back in familiar surroundings. After some hugs and handshakes, we headed home where I was able to have a home-cooked meal and take a shower. The meal never tasted better and the hot shower never felt better. All I wanted to do was put Vietnam behind me and get on with my life. For me, the war was over; I was home, back in the World. I never gave much thought to my buddies, whom I had left behind still fighting the Viet Cong and NVA. This phenomenon was common during the Vietnam War because there was very little unit cohesion during the war.

In reality, the war I thought I had left behind was only just beginning. I was just not aware of it at the time. I had lost a lot of weight during my year in Vietnam and had to be de-wormed when I arrived home. My dad took me to Cleland's Drug Store in WaKeeney, Kansas, to purchase some de-worming medicine. After the first couple of weeks at home, taking the medicine and eating Mom's home-cooked meals, I began to put some weight back on. I was emotionally numb and couldn't talk to anyone about my combat experience, not my family, not my best friend, Dan. I just wanted to sort of isolate myself and take a lot of showers.

I had a month leave at home before I had to report for duty at Fort Stewart, Georgia, to finish out my tour. It wasn't long after I returned home before I was ready to go new car shopping. One day Mom, Dad, and I headed out to look for that new car. We drove to Hays, Salina, Wichita, and Great Bend that day looking for that special car. Toward evening, we arrived in Great Bend on the way back home. Driving by a Chrysler dealership, I glanced into the showroom window and spotted a new 1968 Plymouth Roadrunner, yellow in color with a black roof. I knew right then, there was my dream car. We went into the car dealership, I looked the car over and before we left for home that evening, I was the owner of a new Roadrunner. Beep, Beep! Not too long after I got the new car, I asked Dianne out for a date. We met Dan and his girlfriend, Linda (now his wife), in Hays and went to the drive-in movie theater. As the evening progressed, I became very relaxed and fell asleep.

Author back home from Vietnam with 1968 Roadrunner.

Looking back on that evening, Dianne said, "I remember he was so tired he fell asleep. I remember having mixed emotions about that. Was I not interesting enough to keep him awake? Or, he didn't get any sleep, so therefore he needed the rest (Remember I was 16/17 yrs old). Now that I am older and understand more about life and events involved, I can understand that he was very comfortable with my company and the situation, so that he was able to let his guard down and relax completely."

Dan remembers, "Cruising Main Street constantly in his new car. It was such a unique and hot car and was great to have him home. Cruising Main, drinking beer, shooting pool at Slick's, driving too fast, and celebrating his return seemed great. Unfortunately, I was assuming that we were starting up where we left off before his war ordeal. I did not see the changes he had undergone (except for the weight). I wanted to talk about his war experience, but at a very superficial level. I didn't understand why he did not want to talk about what he had been through, when he had described these experiences in letters to me. The reality was that I was immersed in my college life and he was struggling to right his ship, get out of the military, and build a life after Vietnam."

Not long after I arrived home from Vietnam, I received a letter from my brother, Chuck, who was stationed at Fort Polk, Louisiana.

April 7, 1968

Fort Polk, Louisiana

Dear Wayne,

Well Wayne, I sure was glad to hear you made it home. Have you and Danny had any parties yet? I bet you have. What kind of car have you decided on? I think that a Camaro sounds pretty good to me, but get whatever you like best. We are starting our 1ˢᵗ week of rifle range Monday. We get our first pass in two weeks. I sure will be glad, as we haven't got to leave the company area yet. They sure are being rough on us. I guess that it's for our own good though. Did you see Rick while you were in WaKeeney? I wish that I could have seen him. It sure will be great if you stop by on your way to Fort Stewart. Let me know ahead of time and I'll try to get a pass. Try to make it on a weekend. What's your rank now? Is SP-4 the same as a corporal or what? Tell the folks that I'll try to call home on Easter Sunday. I don't know whether they will let us or not. Well, I better close and get some sleep. Write when you get a chance.

Chuck

I came home from Vietnam with a bad attitude. "What were they going to do, send me back to Nam?" One evening, while home on leave I went to Colby, Kansas, to visit one of my brothers, Ron, who was going to college there at the time. We were cruising around town in the yellow Roadrunner when I noticed red lights flashing in my rearview mirror. The cop pulled me over for some minor traffic violation. As he approached the car, I smarted off to him. "What's your problem?" He promptly had me get out of the vehicle and put me in a spread-eagle position on the hood. Following the pat down, I walked over and got into the patrol car. We started to visit and I told him that I had just returned from Vietnam. He seemed to be understanding and said he knew another soldier who had come home from the war. After a long visit, he let me go without issuing me a ticket.

My thirty-day leave at home was rapidly coming to an end. It had been good being home for awhile before going to Fort Stewart. I was looking forward to finishing my tour of duty and going back to school. I wanted to put my Vietnam experience behind me and get on with my life.

On my way to Fort Stewart, I stopped by Fort Polk in Louisiana to visit with my brother, Chuck. We spent the weekend in New Orleans having a good time. I remember we were slowly driving down Bourbon Street and came to a stop. While stopped, I decided to hold the brake pedal down while stepping on the accelerator, causing the rear tires to squeal and smoke. All of a sudden, I heard a loud thump on the roof of the car. I looked up and there was a huge New Orleans cop staring down at me with a billy club in his hand! I knew I was in trouble, so I stepped on the gas and sped to a side street and headed back to the hotel. Once again, I had managed to dodge a brush with the law.

I arrived at Fort Stewart in May of 1968. It was going to be a long hot summer. The heat and humidity of the Deep South reminded me of where I had just come from: Vietnam. There really wasn't much to do at Fort Stewart. We got off every day at 4:30 p.m. and had to be back no later than midnight. We also had weekends off, which we often used to travel to one of the beautiful beaches in the area.

Demise of the Yellow Roadrunner

My final few months in the Army were going fine until one afternoon when one of my buddies and I decided to take off for Savannah, Georgia, for an evening out on the town. The letter I wrote home to Mom and Dad explaining what happened that night tells the story best. It was not one of my better days, to say the least!

August 18, 1968

Fort Stewart, GA

Dear Mom, Dad and All,

Hi. How's everyone there? I made the report to the insurance company yesterday morning, so am waiting now to see what they do. I sure went and got myself in a jam and it just makes me sick. I'm just glad I didn't happen to be in the car when it happened. This is the way he happened to take my car. I might as well tell you

I'd had quite a bit to drink. Anyway, this girl and I were sitting in my car and the other guy was in the house. I guess he got bored or something and came out and wanted to go see a friend he knew close by. I guess we argued back and forth a few minutes as I didn't want him to take it. Finally, he talked the girl and me to going back into the house and the next thing I knew he was gone. This was about 12 o'clock. At 2 o'clock he got lost and couldn't find the way back to where I was, so he decided to go out to the beach as we have some friends out there. It happened about halfway out there. He claims to have fallen asleep. This was about 4 a.m. I woke up at about 5:30 a.m. and called in to the company to see if he had come back there or they had heard from him. They said he called at 2 a.m. and was lost and that was all they knew, so I decided to wait and see if he would come back and pick me up later in the morning. At about 6 a.m. someone found him. I guess he lay beside the car for about 2 hours. He went off the right side of the road and rolled 5 or 6 times. About 9 a.m., I finally decided that he wasn't coming back, so I took a taxi down to Hunter AFB and had to wait there until 3:30 p.m. for a bus back here to Stewart. I got back here at 5 p.m. and that was when I found out about it. I found out that he doesn't have a driver's license and I really can't say that I gave him permission to take the car, but can't say I didn't either. I guess that's what beer can do to a person. Believe me, this is as close to the truth as I can come or the way I remember it. The other guy may say something else. I have to report to our Company Commander Monday morning. I know if I ever get through this thing, that I will settle down and take care of myself. I doubt if I can get out for school now as this whole mess has to be cleared up before I can get discharged.

Love

Your son,

Wayne

I was honorably discharged from the Army on October 10, 1968. I flew from Savannah, Georgia, to Washington DC to visit my brother Chuck, who was stationed at Fort Meade, Maryland, and also to visit my old roommate, Roger from my college days in Denver. He was in the Army and worked for a general in

Washington DC.

Following a nice visit with them, I flew to Kansas City. As I remember it, I was walking down the street to visit my cousin Sharon, who was attending school there. On the way to see Sharon, I happened to walk by a Chrysler dealership and spotted a bright red 1969 Roadrunner in the show room. I walked in, looked it over, and before the day was out, I was the owner of another new Roadrunner! Beep, Beep! I drove the car back to my hometown of WaKeeney, arriving in the late afternoon. I drove by the high school football field, where my brother Ed was taking part in practice. I caused him to be distracted by my presence, which in turn got him into trouble with the coaching staff. Way to go, Wayne!

In January 1969, I decided to move to Denver once again, this time with my brother Ron and friend Eric. I worked and went to school for about a year before moving back home. I was unsettled and was having a difficult time deciding what to do with my life. In the fall of 1970, I decided to attend Dodge City Community College in Dodge City, Kansas. It was there that I began to settle down. I made new friends, studied hard, and worked part time. Things were beginning to look up; however, there were times I felt very depressed.

In the fall of 1971, starting my second year at DCCC, I met my future wife, Sandy. She was studying to be a nurse. We both had farm backgrounds and seemed to hit it off. After dating for six months, we were married on July 22, 1972, at the First Christian Church in Dodge City.

We decided to come back to the family farm where I helped my dad and Sandy began her nursing career. Eventually, we were able to purchase our own farm. We raised cattle, swine, wheat, and irrigated sorghum and corn. We became the parents of three wonderful children: Troy, Gina, and Royce. I was keeping very busy, but Vietnam was always there, lurking in the background.

The farming operation was going well until the early 1980s when interest rates skyrocketed and land values plummeted. We were in a no-win situation and by the late 1980s had lost most of our farm and were forced into bankruptcy. In August of 1986, to make ends meet and provide for my family, I took a job at the Trego County Highway Department. I didn't like the job, but I had to do something to make a living. Because both Sandy and I worked in WaKeeney and our children attended school there, we decided to move off the farm in January 1986 to a house closer to town.

In the spring of 1990, I noticed that the Vietnam Veterans Memorial Moving Wall was coming to a nearby town. I knew I needed to visit it, so on a Friday evening, I took my family to Ness City, Kansas, to see the memorial, which I'd heard was a moving experience. As I looked at the wall, remembering my buddies who had died in Vietnam, I became very emotional. For years, I had put off dealing with this part of my life. Now, I was standing there, staring it in the face. There were the names of men I had known and was with when they died. It was overwhelming. Tears ran down my cheeks. I had been caught off guard and was not prepared for this moment.

I thought my Vietnam experience was behind me, but unbeknownst to me, it was only beginning. It was like a slow awakening at first. As time went on, I began to remember things that had happened that I had never talked to anyone about. I wanted to know more about Vietnam and by 1994 had decided that I needed to make a return trip to see the country again. It had seemed like a nightmare while I was there during the war. I had been able to block out my war experiences all these years, but now I had to face them.

In March of 1995, I joined nine other veterans and one spouse on a thirteen-day journey back to Vietnam. One of my goals was to meet a former enemy. During the war, the enemy seemed to be invisible. You very rarely saw the Viet Cong or NVA during a firefight. They had the advantage, fighting the war on their own turf.

On one of my first nights back in Vietnam, at the Rex Hotel in Ho Chi Minh City (formerly Saigon) where we were staying, I met Nguyen van Nghia, a former North Vietnamese Army Lieutenant and his family from Tien Hai, a village near Hanoi. Our Vietnamese tour guide was not with us; however, the veterans from opposite sides of the war, the United States and North Vietnam, spent thirty minutes together, ending the evening with a toast of friendship.

Author and Steve Smith with Nguyen van Nghia (center) and family at the Rex Hotel in Ho Chi Minh City.

I was seeing the country in a whole new light. The people were friendly and outgoing. I was able to travel to some of the places where I had been stationed during the war. Everything had changed. Visiting the area where Camp Radcliff had been located during the war near An Khe in the Central Highlands, I found very little left, only some concrete helicopter landing pads. The whole area was grassed over; you would never have known there had been a division base camp there thirty years ago. Traveling on north from Qui Nhon to Danang along National Highway 1, we made stops at Bong Son, LZ English, and LZ Uplift. These LZs were staging areas for the 1st Cavalry Division and 173rd Airborne Brigade. The locals use the airstrip at LZ English for drying rice. When we arrived at LZ English, there were few people around. Within ten minutes of our arrival, the word must have spread, as about 100 children crowded around our bus. I have a picture of children stealing boxes of C-rations at LZ English in June, 1967. It was a very rewarding experience this time to give out candy.

While in Danang, we spent one day relaxing at China Beach, an R & R hot spot for GIs during the war. We also spent one day touring the Marble Mountain cave complex, the Cham Museum, and downtown Danang. We had lunch at Bob Christie's Harbourside Restaurant. He is a New Zealander who serves American-style food, which we were all looking forward to. It was great to have a hamburger and fries. From Bob Christie's we went to a place that served Five Snake wine. A few of us tried it. Not too bad! The next day we departed for Hue (pop. 200,000).

Hue served as Vietnam's political capital from 1802 to 1945 under the thirteen emperors of the Nguyen Dynasty. Traditionally, the city has been one of Vietnam's cultural, religious, and educational centers. Today, Hue's main attractions are the splendid tombs of the Nguyen Emperors, several notable pagodas, and the remains of the Citadel. While in Hue, we also took a day trip to the former Khe Sanh combat base, site of the most famous siege of the Vietnam War. On another day trip, we went to explore the Ben Hai River/DMZ area, including the McNamara Line, Quang Tri, and old Marine and Army bases. My overall impression of Vietnam in 1995 was that of a country very much at peace.

I came home from Vietnam in 1995 with a much different view of the country. While I was stationed there in the late 1960s, it was a nightmare. I was nineteen, green, and scared with an M-16. By 1995 the country had changed drastically. It had gone from wartime to peacetime. The economy had grown, and the Vietnamese people were better off. The United States was in the process of re-establishing ties with the Vietnamese people. On July 11, 1995, President William J. Clinton announced the normalization of relations with Vietnam.[15]

The trip to Vietnam, in 1995 was healing and brought some peace of mind, but still there were missing pieces to the puzzle I was trying to put together. In the summer of 1996, I learned that Nguyen Van Nghia, the former North Vietnamese Army lieutenant, was being brought to Dallas, Texas, from his home in Vietnam for surgery on his war wounds. In November 1996, Nghia arrived in Dallas and I was there at the Dallas-Fort Worth airport to help welcome him to the United States.

That weekend in Dallas changed my life. My friend Barry Six, whom I had met on the 1995 trip to Vietnam, came up from his home in Austin to join me. We had a long talk about our war experiences, and, as we talked, he began saying things that I had been feeling for a long time. As he talked about Post-Traumatic Stress Disorder, I was finally able to put a name with the way I was feeling and acting. I had never heard of PTSD, but in the next few weeks, I came to the realization that I did indeed suffer from it.

On January 6, 1997, I drove to the Colmery-O'Neil VA hospital in Topeka seeking help. After checking in and waiting around for several hours, I was directed to see the VFW service officer at the VA. He suggested that I should file a claim for Post-Traumatic Stress Disorder with the VA. After waiting several months, I received a letter from the VA one day, awarding me a 70 percent disability for PTSD. In May, 1997, I sent an application to the director of the PTSD Readjustment Treatment Program and was soon accepted for treatment.

What is Post-Traumatic Stress Disorder?

Post-Traumatic Stress Disorder has existed since man first began fighting wars. PTSD has been described as the normal reaction of a normal person to abnormal circumstances. PTSD is a set of symptoms that surface after a dangerous, frightening, and uncontrollable traumatic event.

PTSD has had many names from past wars: shell shock, war neurosis, and battle fatigue are some of the most common. PTSD symptoms fall into four categories: Avoidance—amnesia, disassociation, numbing, hyper vigilance, controlling behavior, and isolation; Reliving—flashbacks, sleep disorders, overwhelming feelings, and overacting; Victimization—distrust, abandonment, helplessness, fear of change, and blaming others; and Shame—feeling guilty, feeling as if you're crazy, and feeling unworthy.

Entering PTSD Readjustment Treatment Program

In August of 1997, I entered a ninety-day in-patient readjustment treatment program for Post-Traumatic Stress Disorder at the Colmery-O'Neal Veterans Administration Medical Center in Topeka, Kansas. I benefitted a lot from this intense program designed to help veterans who suffer from PTSD.

When I entered the readjustment treatment program, I was running out of gas, so to speak. I was suffering from a high level of stress and knew I needed some help dealing with my combat experiences. I had lost my "peace of mind" and was continually bothered by memories of traumatic events that occurred during my tour of duty in Vietnam. I felt detached and disconnected from others and had the inability to recall important aspects of traumatic events, such as the Tet Offensive of 1968. I had trouble sleeping, poor concentration, difficulty with anger, and irritability; I felt on guard much of the time.

I had been able to block out my combat experiences for twenty-two years, but it wasn't working anymore. I had thought about committing suicide in the years prior to my admission into the readjustment treatment program and had even planned how I would do it. I knew in my heart that suicide was not the answer to escape the mental anguish I was experiencing. I thought of my family and friends and what a selfish act this would be and what it would do to them.

My first couple of weeks in the PTSD readjustment treatment program were stressful, but as time went on and I become acquainted with other vets in the program, I felt more at ease. The doctors, nurses, and staff treated me with respect and dignity. I missed my family and home, but I knew I needed to complete the program for a better life.

I was given a thorough physical examination and prescribed medications to address my PTSD symptoms and other physical ailments. I began attending psychotherapy group sessions three times a week. There were six to eight veterans in each group. The session was supervised by a VA doctor and usually lasted fifty minutes. We were encouraged to talk about how our treatment was going and any other thoughts or issues we wanted to share with the group. The psychotherapy group sessions were helpful and gave me insight in understanding my own psyche.

Later in the program, I attended trauma group sessions. My group was very small; there were three of us and the doctor. Deep down, I had a lot of anger over past events. Witnessing the death of my comrades and innocent Vietnamese civilians left my young mind filled with conflict and grief. The purpose of the trauma group was to allow veterans to open up and share their most inner personal feelings regarding their traumas in a safe environment.

One day during trauma group, I brought Lee Danielson's etching from the Vietnam Veterans Memorial Wall in Washington DC. It was my turn to talk about my traumas and Lee in particular. I needed to release my hurt and anger, realize that I had no control over these events, and that I needed to accept what happened and move on. When the trauma group sessions ended, I arranged a healing ceremony with the VA chaplain, Father Jim Moster, for our group.

We held the ceremony in the VA Chapel. To begin the ceremony, each of us wrote down on a piece of paper what we were ready to let go of. We then approached the altar and placed our messages of pained desperation in a container, lit a match, and burned the paper, thereby bringing a fitting and respectful closure to those things that had bothered us the most over the past years. Father Jim then prayed for our healing and reconciliation with God. Father Jim said, "God takes care of those things we can't, and we trust him to bring healing and goodness out of this closure." Following the ceremony, we went outside the chapel and buried the ashes.

During my time at the VA hospital, I received many cards, letters, and visits from family and friends. That show of support meant a lot to me and gave me something to look forward to each day. Toward the end of my stay at the hospital, I wrote a veterans summary of progress treatment report: "I am beginning to feel more relaxed and in control of my emotions. I believe the reason for this is I am more aware of things going on around me and I am making a conscious effort to be more relaxed and let things happen, rather than trying to take control." After three months of treatment, I graduated and returned home.

One day, three years after completing the program, I was at the Topeka VA to attend PCT (Post-Traumatic Stress Disorder Clinical Team), an out-patient program for veterans. Walking down the hallways of the VA, I happened to meet Father Jim Moster, the chaplain at the hospital. I believed he had given me good counsel during my treatment in 1997. I was starting to formulate my book idea and thought he could help, so I asked him for an interview, and he graciously accepted.

(Transcribed from taped interview)

Wayne: The experience of combat affects a person's soul and spirituality. I am looking for some answers. I thought maybe you could give me some insight.

Father Jim: Right, the experience of trauma creates an experience which is so overwhelming, so powerful that it becomes an all-absorbing thing in your overall life and the experience of the individual who has been traumatized. The experience then becomes the focus of thought, feeling, awareness, and sense of well-being: all the spiritual components of the person are totally absorbed and caught up and focused on the reaction to the traumatic event. Therefore, the reaction formation is so powerful that it becomes the total experience, outlook, and focus of the traumatized person.

The reaction formation robs the individual of the freedom to experience a full range of feelings, thoughts, and spiritual awareness of the individual who has been traumatized. It's overwhelming and overpowering and therefore becomes domineering. There is much more to a person than any one set of thoughts, memories, or feelings. The trick in dealing with recovery from trauma is to desensitize the individual who has been traumatized to that reaction formation into that original traumatic experience, so that he or she can get some distance from that and reactivate their feelings in other areas of their life.

It then creates a greater freedom for the individual who has been traumatized to experience themselves in their life and their relationship to other people and to their world.

All that gets bound up and overly focused in the reaction formation of trauma. The spiritual component of that, of course is, first of all, awareness of how they are being affected by their trauma. Taking charge of the reaction formations, not allowing them to be always triggered so that they can be aware of what triggers them. They can choose to avoid those triggers that automatically thrust them right back into the whole experience of the trauma and thus rob them of their freedom. To help them reestablish their belief system and the methods by which they can achieve a sense of well-being and a sense of peace at the center of their soul.

Wayne: How do you look at God if you have been in combat and you have taken part in killing people? I have some guilt about that. Some were innocent, some were the enemy, but still, they were human beings. To be involved in killing and seeing the aftermath, I don't know where I stand before God.

Father Jim: There would be two components to deal with—overall in treating guilt surrounding trauma. One is to carefully understand the debilitating nature of fear, orders, rage, and anger at being caught in an impossible situation. Being under orders to carry out a mission that requires what they're doing, being aware they were not free to act as they did because of fear, rage, and being put into an impossible, hopeless, and meaningless situation. Recognizing that you don't have responsibility for what you did because you were not free when you did those things. Your freedom of choice was almost nothing. You had no choice.

What was in play here was the role of fear, the role of anger, and the role of responsibility to yourself and to your buddies, the whole role of survival. Survival is a natural instinct, it's probably the strongest instinct we have. When you are put into a position where your very existence is being threatened, the law of instinct takes over. You cannot rationalize that out, you cannot overcome it, and you simply act to preserve your life and that of others who are helping you.

Sometimes the rage involved in it, the impossibility of the situation, the fear—all of that combined—caused people to do things they would never dream of doing when they are calm and not in such a high stress situation.

Wayne: That's one of the problems I'm having—reconciling with the past. Today, I cannot imagine doing something like we did back thirty-some years ago.

Father Jim: If you were put into the same situation that you were in at the time of your trauma, the time that you're feeling guilty about, you probably would have done the same as you did or worse. Any human being is capable of that kind of behavior when their options are cut off and they're put into an impossible situation. So to see yourself as being responsible—needing to be responsible—to make up for that. Seeing yourself as someway inferior, or worse than other people, because of what you did is really not a fair assessment of the reality of who you are.

You're a human being and you did a job that any human being would have done in much the same way if they were put into the same situation. The other piece of treating guilt issues is looking at your concept of God. The concept of God is one that you learned early in life. It is one that's pretty restricted. It's bound by laws, regulations, and rules. It's one that's conditioned on punishment and reward. That is usually a pretty infantile understanding of God. It's a limited understanding of the nature of God. So the experience of trauma and the experience of our own behavior under extremely stressful conditions—to look at our behavior under those conditions would cause us to really judge ourselves harshly.

We would have to come to the conclusion that either we are impossibly or hopelessly evil ourselves for what we did or there is no God. If there is a God, and he is as we learned him [to be] early in life, then we are in an impossible situation. We are up for annihilation; we are up for severe punishment, and so what we have to do is grow in our understanding of who God is. He is bigger than we learned, a much bigger entity, a much bigger reality, more benevolent and broader in his dealings with us than our eighteen, nineteen, twenty-year-old concept and understanding of him has left us with. So we have to broaden and expand our understanding of who God actually is.

Wayne: That is one of the issues that a lot of guys have to deal with. When you grew up, your family went to church and you learned about God and Christ. The number one issue is that "Thou shalt not kill." Then before you're even twenty years old you're out killing people.

Father Jim: Right, right, that's a tremendous conflict for a young person. Young people seventeen, eighteen, nineteen, twenty years old and younger always follow the law, and everything is black and white. The older we become, unless we have been stunted by trauma in our development, in our emotional and spiritual development, we grow beyond and we see that the law is not all black and white, that the law doesn't apply the same in every circumstance.

There are always exceptions. There are always higher values that can be violated even by being true to the commandments. For instance, as an example, the law of love is the highest law. If I did not exert myself to defend a helpless woman or child who is being attacked or threatened by somebody because I might hurt somebody or I might kill somebody, then I am following the law as I learned it as a child. But I'm really not a very mature adult because I'm not looking at the bigger picture.

It's more important for me to follow the law of love and the law of reason, which says the life and safety of this woman or child is much more important than whether or not my helping them, by defending them, is going to result in someone's death. So, under normal circumstances people do grow. One of the effects of trauma is that it crystallizes your spiritual development at the age at which the trauma happened. Usually, that is a pretty young age when you are in combat.

Wayne: Do you mean like shatter?

Father Jim: No, it crystallizes it in the sense that it stops growth. That's where you are stuck. You don't develop spiritually anymore. As a result, what you're doing is looking back thirty years later. You are looking at yourself and judging yourself for what you did under impossible circumstances. You are judging yourself by an impossible set of rules and regulations, that is, "Thou shalt not kill." That's impossible in a combat situation. It's impossible in a traumatic situation in which survival is paramount, where you are not free to act as a human being in relationship to the law that you know is correct.

So you transgress the law, but still you are trying to hold yourself responsible. The only way around that is to understand what the reality was, what the reality of God is. That he is bigger than that, and [then you need to] work on your growth of understanding that God is not irrational. He does not expect us to be responsible for things that are way beyond our control.

There are a lot of powerful issues that have to be talked about and dealt with in coming to a true perspective on that. A lot of it comes down to letting go and trusting in God and also recognizing that you are still here. You are enjoying a lot of benefits and blessings that are obviously coming from somewhere. Does God bless those he is trying to punish? Is he that kind of God? I don't think so. If he is the kind of God who holds strict justice and he holds you accountable only to the Ten Commandments under all circumstances, then all of us are in an impossible situation. [You need to get] all of this into perspective and recognize that there is a bigger reality than just the Ten Commandments.

Wayne: The reality is the memory is so ingrained in me that I can see those people lying there dead that we had just killed. I just cannot get that out of my mind.

Father Jim: One of the tools around dealing with guilt is, one of the psychological tools that were taught to you in the program here, is the awareness of the role of thinking in triggers and in your feelings. We can take charge of what we choose to think about. We can choose to fill our mind with thoughts that are productive, that are pleasant, and that are different than those things that are so powerfully there to claim our attention when we don't have anything that we are consciously focusing on.

In other words, nature will not tolerate a vacuum. If I don't fill my mind with positive thoughts of my own choosing, then the memories that are very powerful from the past will fill my consciousness, and those thoughts will claim and take over. So I have to learn how to ignore, catch myself when I'm starting to think about things that I know are going to really take me over. I have to recognize that as soon as it's starting, and I have to learn techniques for filling my mind with things that I choose, that I know are not going to trigger me back into those guilty feelings and those memories and experiences that are so vivid in my past. Does that make sense?

Wayne: Yes it does. I do a lot of activities to try and do what you are saying, but there is some part of me that won't let go of all this. I just cannot let go of it. Most of the time, I feel pretty good. I have been working the last few weeks getting our hunting lodge in shape, our old house we used to live in, getting it all fixed up for the guys to come out and hunt pheasants this Saturday. I have been focusing on that recently. There's just something there I'm dealing with I can't let go of.

Father Jim: Is it something that you talked about and dealt with in trauma group sessions or psychotherapy?

Wayne: Yes, in trauma group, I think I probably dealt with it. It's just something I don't want to let go of. It comes down to the very fact that my financial support comes from the VA.

Father Jim: You are suspecting that if you let go of that…

Wayne: That's part of it.

Father Jim: That's a common thing that does complicate your being able to get freedom from that. It complicates it.

Wayne: It does.

Father Jim: It really does. That's because you're an honest person and you are very honest and you know that, but I would say in response to that even though you let go of it, the compensation that you're getting is nothing compared to what you should be getting. The fact that you have been traumatized and those memories are there and what you have been through, there is no way that our country could pay you enough to reimburse you for what you went through.

So, I wouldn't think you need to feel guilty about getting free of the effects of trauma as much as you can and also having your compensation. There is no way that the compensation you are getting from the government could ever repay you for what you suffered and went through.

So, you don't need to maintain symptoms, you don't need to maintain any kind of mechanism inside of yourself that's going to cause you pain over this in order to justify your service-connected compensation. I really don't think that is an issue, except maybe in your own heart and mind. You feel if you get free of the effects of PTSD, that you don't deserve being compensated. I think it is not probably a judgment that I would make, at least.

Wayne: There is no cure for PTSD?

Father Jim: No, you will never be cured. If you can manage that illness, minimize the pain, negativity, and the negative influence on your life and your freedom, that's the thing to do. You're not going to cure the illness. You're never going to be fully free of PTSD, but that doesn't keep you from managing PTSD as well as you can to the greatest freedom, the greatest happiness you can have now, for the rest of your life.

You need to manage that. The government is not paying you for how much pain you have. They're paying you for damages that have already been done and cannot be reversed. That's what the compensation is for. Nobody can pay you for the pain. So the idea is, to get rid of the pain as much as possible or manage it using the tools that you have learned here. The only way to get free of guilt is to let go of it. The means of letting go of it is to share it with at least one human being. You have to talk about it. You have to get it out. You have to talk about it openly and freely.

Wayne: What happened to me, I was totally unaware that I had PTSD until about four years ago. I had no idea, and I had to tell somebody some of the stuff that happened, so I went to our pastor. I belong to the United Methodist Church. The pastor deals with people who have been traumatized. When I first talked about it, I just about broke down every time I tried to talk about it.

Father Jim: Sure.

Wayne: First time, I had never told the details to anyone. He was the first one I ever told the details to, of some of the stuff I remembered. I'm at the point that now I am pretty comfortable talking about it.

Father Jim: That's good, and it doesn't hurt to keep talking about it with people that you can trust.

Wayne: I'm at the point now I try to find something to look forward to each day. Maybe someday I will write a book.

Father Jim: That's a good point. You know, having something that's important to your life, a goal to focus on and to invest yourself in, fills that empty space that normally will be taken over naturally by past experiences, memories, and feelings. If you don't have something to fill that space and time, then things from the past will come rushing in to fill that void.

One way of putting it: if you have polluted water in a lake behind a dam, there is a lot of pressure on that dam. If there's no support for that dam on the other side and the polluted water keeps flowing in and filling it up, eventually it will break the dam through, and you are going to have problems.

One answer to that is to bolster the strength of the dam, to keep the pollution in its place, fill the other side with good water. You fill the other side of the dam with good water, it will counterbalance the pressure on the other side and keep the bad stuff where it belongs and allow the good stuff to be there and be able to focus on that.

So, the idea is to fill your life with things that you feel are wholesome, good, and important to you now and that will be the good water on the side of the dam that will keep the others back and keep it in its place, keep it contained.

Wayne: I do feel very lucky compared to some veterans I know. I have a really great family and I've got a wonderfully close friend. (Author's note: End of interview)

After completing the in-patient readjustment treatment program at the VA hospital, I began to feel like I had a new lease on life. Talking to other veterans who had experiences similar to my own was helpful. The psychotherapy and trauma group sessions allowed me to express my feelings and emotions in a safe environment. I now felt ready to go back out and face the world.

In December of 1997, the VA granted me entitlement to individual unemployability, and I was awarded a 100 percent rating for my service-connected disability: PTSD.

In the summer of 1998, at the age of fifty, I decided to once again take up running after a long layoff. I had always enjoyed running. I originally took up running in 1984, completing two marathons that year. In 1986, I decided to try to run across Kansas, from the Nebraska border to the Oklahoma border to raise funds for the Trego County Fair grandstands. The grandstand was in bad shape and needed to be replaced. The attempt failed miserably, as I only made it a little over the fourth of the way to Oklahoma. I had a lot to learn about long distance running. During the next few years, I ran numerous 10Ks and other shorter races.

Daily exercise was very helpful in controlling my PTSD symptoms along with the medications that the VA gave me. It wasn't long after I started running again that I decided to run a marathon. I set my sights on the Chicago Marathon in October and began training for the 26.2-mile race. My goal was to finish the race in less than five hours. I decided to run for a cause, so I chose the American Cancer Society. After four months of training, I felt ready and fit to tackle the Chicago

Marathon.

For support, my friend Dan accompanied me to Chicago for the big weekend. I ended up finishing in just a little over five hours, not quite reaching my goal. Crossing the finish line gave me a feeling of exhilaration despite some painful blisters I acquired along the way. After a few days of resting my sore muscles, the satisfaction of realizing I had finished the 26.2-mile race and raised over $1000.00 for the American Cancer Society took over. From 1999 through 2006, I ran and finished twelve more marathons including the New York City Marathon and Dublin Ireland Marathon. I also ran two ultra-marathons, the JFK 50 Mile race in Boonsboro, Maryland, and the Heartland 50 Mile race in Cassoday, Kansas.

During the fall of 1998, I felt the need to return to Vietnam once again, this time on a solo journey. I began making plans to travel to Hanoi. I wanted to visit the northern part of the country and to participate in the Toyota Friendship Half-Marathon, a 13.1-mile race, which I thought would be a fun event. I also made arrangements to meet Nguyen van Nghia and his wife while in Hanoi.

On Wednesday morning, November 18, 1998, I arrived at the Hanoi Noi Bai Airport. I felt some apprehension around the Vietnamese security guards who looked serious, but soon I met my tour guide, Mr. Le Hien, and driver and began to relax. From the airport we drove to the Chains First Eden Hotel where I would be staying for the next week.

The first couple of days I spent sightseeing around the city, visiting the One Pillar Pagoda, the Dien Huu Pagoda, and the Temple of Literature. I also visited Ho Chi Minh's Stilt House. One evening, I took in the theater, attending a Vietnamese water puppets program. Vietnamese water puppets were invented a thousand years ago by farmers in the Red River Delta region near Hanoi to entertain themselves when the rains flooded their rice paddy fields. The theater has presented performances in various international festivals and carries out cultural exchange activities with other countries. The program, which was one hour long with seventeen acts, was a pleasant way to spend the warm November evening.

I soon became acclimated to Hanoi and its people. The northern Vietnamese are friendly, but more reserved than the people in the south. The city is quite lively, with motorbikes, bicycles, and a few cars traveling in every direction. Crossing the street was a challenge, until my tour guide and interpreter, Hien, advised me to keep walking and not stop. Otherwise, he warned, I might get run over. It took some practice, but I managed to learn the art of crossing a street in Hanoi.

Hien, who would now be forty-five, was seven when the Christmas bombings by the Americans took place at the end of 1972. He told me he had vivid memories of the bombings. He spoke English fairly well, but there were times I couldn't understand what he was trying to tell me.

One morning Nguyen van Nghia, the former North Vietnamese Lieutenant I had met during my 1995 trip to Vietnam, and his wife came to the hotel for a short visit. We had a pleasant time together (with the help of my interpreter Hien) over coffee and some picture-taking in the park across the street from the hotel. I had planned to accompany Nghia back to his village in Tien Hai, but due to some tensions in the area, foreigners were advised not to go there, so I had to change my plans.

That afternoon, I asked Hien if he could take me to a children's orphanage. He agreed to, and so we traveled to the southern part of Hanoi and stopped at the Birla Children's Village. There, I met Chu Dinh Diep, the director of the village, and was offered green tea, which I gladly accepted. Drinking green tea is a custom in Vietnam when welcoming visitors. We had a pleasant conversation concerning the children at the village. I inquired about the possibility of sponsoring a student to attend college. The director said that he would talk it over with orphanage staff and choose a promising candidate.

Author poses with children at Birla Children's Village.

Later that afternoon, I visited the infamous Hanoi Hilton, where U.S.

POWs were kept during the American War, as people in the north refer to it. Today, the old prison is a museum with special emphasis on showing how political prisoners were treated in the 1930s by the French.

On the fourth day, I took a day trip to the Perfume Pagoda, located about sixty kilometers southwest of Hanoi. Getting to the pagoda requires a journey first by road, which takes about two hours from Hanoi to My Duc, then by small boat rowed by two women for one hour to the foot of the mountain. The scenery was magnificent as the boat made its way up the river, with majestic mountains on both sides. The view of the river and boat ride was very calm and peaceful.

After I got off the boat, it was a two-hour walk to the main gate of the pagoda. The Perfume Pagoda itself is a complex of pagodas and Buddhist shrines built into the limestone cliffs of Huong Tich Mountain.

My fifth and last full day in Hanoi began early as I traveled across the city to the starting point of the Toyota Friendship Half Marathon, which I had entered. As the start of the race approached, I tried to prepare myself mentally, not knowing if I had fully recovered from the Chicago Marathon I had run a few weeks earlier. The purpose of the 13.1-mile half-marathon was to promote friendship and improve the level of athletics in Vietnam.

I was one of sixty-eight foreign runners from twelve countries, including the United States, Japan, England, China, France, Holland, and Canada, which added to the race's cosmopolitan diversity and underscored the event's emphasis on international goodwill and friendship. There were 1,684 participants in the event's various races, including the children's race, the 10K, and the half marathon.

My race started off well enough as we made two laps around Hoan Kiem Lake and then headed north and then west by Truc Bach Lake and West Lake. As I approached the sixteen-kilometer marker (about ten miles) near the Ho Chi Minh Mausoleum, I began to have trouble running. By the time I reached the nineteenth kilometer (about twelve miles), a race official on a motorcycle came along and waved at me to stop.

They had imposed a two-hour time limit to finish the race, which I was totally unaware of. I was exhausted and had painful blisters on my feet. Tears of disappointment came to my eyes as I realized I would not be allowed to finish the race. The race official on the motorcycle motioned for me to jump on the back of the cycle, and he took me to the finish area. By the time we reached the finish line, I felt better; I realized it had been fun and exciting to be a participant in this international event. Some 400,000 people had lined the race route to show support and give encouragement to the runners. The people were quite friendly, and the children waved as I passed them.

Author running through the streets of Hanoi.

I met some interesting people on the trip, including a group from Holland who traveled somewhere in the world annually to run a marathon. There was also a professor from the University of Sydney, Australia, whom I met in the hotel and was in Vietnam doing agricultural research.

Soon after arriving back in the United States, I received a letter from the Birla Children's Village informing me of the student they had chosen for me to sponsor. He was seventeen-year-old Pham Viet Kha.

The Birla Children's village Hanoi
Mai Dich – small town
Cau Giay – district
Hanoi City – Vietnam

Hanoi   December 9, 1998

Dear: Wayne Purinton
RR 1 Box 3
WaKeeney, KS 67672-9701

On behalf of all staffs and 78 orphans in the Birla children's village Hanoi, I wish you and your family good health, happiness and achievement.

It is our pleasure to receive your letter and your gift (on 1st Dec 1998). I received the donation of 120 USD from you to the orphans in our village.

I said with you: the staffs and all the children got together on after received you gift. The children discussed then elect Pham Viet Kha. He was born in Nov 23rd 1981. He is a orphan. He is in grade 12nd in Hermann Gmeiner school.

We report about Kha to you: Kha is oldest brother in his family, good activities, observe working discipline. All people at home love him very much. When Kha was in grade 10th. We often mobilize his study. He tried good at school. He always learn on his own and study after work. The tuition refund a month is 20 USD. When Kha receive your gift He very happy. He promises to learn well so repay for your help and all.

We send your cheque onto the bank (21 days after send onto bank, money can draw from the bank).

We thank for your help. We look forward to seeing you again in the Birla children's village. We wish you achievement, good health. We would appreciate highly your attention and assistance to the Birla children's village and others. We give you a Kha's photo.

Your sincerely,
Deputy Director
Chu Dinh Diep

Pham Viet Kah, left, and Chu Dinh Diep, right.

Hanoi December 9, 1998

<u>Dear:</u> *Wayne Purinton*

RR 1 Box 3

WaKeeney, KS 67672-9701

I would like to introduce myself. My full name is Pham Viet Kha. I have lived in Birla children's village for 6 years. I am in grade 12th in Hermann Gmeiner school. I know that the 12nd grade is very important. I must final examination and into University. I must try more myself. I must learn on my own and to study after work so that review the all lessons.

Although every people love me very much but the tuition refund isn't enough to pay for me. With love from the Leaders in the Birla who must beg money to help me.

I received 20USD/a month from you. It is over great with me. I would like to thank for you help. I have never seen you, but I always believe that you are a kindness man. I wish you good health, happiness, achievement in your life. I promise to try to learn well so that repay for your help and all people.

Your sincerely,

Pham Viet Kha

Hanoi December 2, 1999

Dear Wayne Purinton

I'm Pham Viet Kha in Birla children's village. The first, I would like to ask your health and your family. How are you? Have you practiced to run? Have you taken part in running events?

I hope that you are still well and running every day. I would like to thank for you help to me during longtime ago.

I spent the money for my practicing Mathematics, Physics, Chemistry and Informatics. I have finished 12ᵗʰ grade and reviewing lessons into University. I understand that into University very difficult with me and that's very important in my life. I'm still believe that I'll pass.

I want that next time I'll receive your sponsor for my study. I hope that you always keep your health and practicing everyday and to have many awards.

Your faithfully,

Pham Viet Kha

October 12, 2000

Dear Wayne,

Today, I have received your letter through Mr. Diep. I have known your good idea with me. I would like to thank for your help.

In your letter I have known that you and your family still good health and you are still running every day. I am glad.

Now I am studying in the first year of Computer Department in National Economy University. I had left the Birla village, so my life is very hard. Your help not only help material but also to encourage spirit for me.

If you are really to come to Vietnam three years, I will meet you. I hope, you'll give to me your address so that I can visit you. I wish you and your family good health. I am very happy when after running match, I can see your photograph shape to take Cup in your arms like the photograph you presented to me. I would like hearing from you.

Your faithfully,

Pham Viet Kha

Hanoi

May 15, 2001

Today, I write this letter to you. I would like to ask your health. How are you? I should have written to you before time, but have a lot of things to do. I'm really busy, you forgive for me.

I have finished the military training and to have result in the first term. I'm average in class with to sum up marks is 6,3 / 10. In next term I must try more.

When I finish the second term, I plan a visit to my native village and you? Summer coming. What do you plan? I think that, the places if you visit, they're very beautiful. I hope you have good holiday. I wish you and your family good health. I promise to write to you soon.

Your sincerely,

Pham Viet Kha

Hanoi   May 14, 2002

Dear Wayne,

It was a great pleasure to receive your letter. I hope you are well and successful. I am going to pass the second examination of the second year. This year I have learnt limited specialty subjects so I am harder than the first year – average mark in the first term of the second year is 6, 3 / 10. It's not good but in the second term I must try more. In the morning I get up early then I play football. I think that to play football to run in order to training for good health. I would like to wish you good health and running ever.

Your

Pham Viet Kha

P.S. Mr. Diep has received your letter and cheque in May 13, 2002.

Hanoi May 23, 2002

Dear: Mr. Wayne Purinton

It was a great pleasure to receive your letter and your Cheque sending to Kha. I would like to wish you and all the very best of good health, happy. Please give your wife and your children our sincere best wishes. Are you still running? I hope next time you'll come to Vietnam and to visit us.

We are well, 110 children in my village are well – behaved and hard working. Kha is in the second year of University, at that time Kha has examination for the end of the second term. Kha is well-behaved, he always visits us and his mother house. He makes progress in his studies. We often check his study in University. Every month Kha returns Village and to ask for his school fees. We wish you good health and always miss us.

THE BIRLA CHILDREN'S VILLAGE HANOI

VICE DIRECTOR

CHU DINH DIEP

.

CHAPTER TWENTY-ONE

Humanitarian Aid Mission Trip

Even though I had been back to Vietnam twice since the war, I still had a yearning to return one more time. On my first two trips, I had been a tourist on a mission to see and explore this once war-torn country. There was something more than being a tourist, however, that I felt I needed to do. I was feeling an urge go back, but this time, I would help make a difference.

One day, while reading *The Veteran,* a magazine published by the Vietnam Veterans of America, I noticed an ad about an organization that financed projects and sent teams of veterans, family members, and others to Vietnam to help construct clinics, houses for disabled veterans, vocational training centers, and kindergarten classrooms. The organization was called the Veterans Vietnam Restoration Project. It sounded like something I would like to be a part of. Here was an organization, started by Vietnam veterans, who were going back and making a difference in the lives of the Vietnamese people.

Over a period of time, I came to the conclusion that perhaps this was the organization I had in mind for another return trip back to Vietnam. I was looking for a spiritual healing and cleansing for my soul. Giving back and helping others less fortunate than myself would be a way to accomplish my goal of reconciling with the Vietnamese people. I had witnessed a lot of death and destruction in

Vietnam during my tour of duty. It made me realize how short and precious life really can be.

My decision to join Veterans Vietnam Restoration Project came in May of 2008, almost a year before the start of the project in A Ngo Commune, A Luoi, Vietnam. Once I had made the decision to join and had been accepted as a VVRP team member, months of anticipation and planning followed. I needed to update my passport and get all of the necessary vaccinations to travel in Southeast Asia. We purchased our airline tickets six months in advance of our March 31, 2009 departure date. My return date was April 22.

Time crept along; first it was months away, and then weeks, then days. As the time neared to return to a country I once couldn't wait to leave, I realized I couldn't wait to go back. One day, it occurred to me I would be leaving home destined for Vietnam on March 26, 2009, the same day I left for Vietnam forty-two years earlier, March 26, 1967. That coincidence seemed a little uncanny.

The Journey

When the day finally arrived to begin the journey back to Vietnam, a problem arose. I needed to travel to Denver International Airport, about 300 miles west of my home. The weather forecast was calling for blizzard conditions in the Denver vicinity, causing concern as to whether I would make it to the airport and catch my flight to San Francisco the next morning. Sure enough, the further west I traveled along Interstate 70, the worse the road conditions became. Driving the last ninety miles into Denver, I experienced slick, snow packed roads, making for a slow, treacherous drive. I finally arrived at the hotel where I was staying near the airport, with a sigh of relief. I was going to make my flight after all.

Arriving in San Francisco the next afternoon, I traveled by bus to Sebastopol, the site of VVRP team training. At the bus drop-off site, I was greeted by Scott Rutherford, VVRP board member/coordinator, and Bud Bruton, also a VVRP board member. Bud was returning on his third VVRP mission, having been a member of Teams XVIII and XXII. As things turned out, Bud and I would be roommates during our trip to Vietnam. Bud is a very likable guy, and we got along fine during the trip. During his tour of duty in Vietnam, Bud flew an L-19/O-1 Bird Dog, which is a liaison and observation aircraft. Bud served with the 220th

Reconnaissance Airplane Company. Their area of operation was the northern I Corp, extending from North of the Hai Van Pass to the DMZ and west to the Laotian border, which included Khe Sanh and the A Shau Valley and East to the South China Sea. The 220th unit call sign was Catkillers. Bud's call sign was Catkiller 18.

For team training, we stayed at former VVRP team member Gene Power's home. Here, we underwent an intense three-day orientation and team-building workshop. It was facilitated by two volunteers, Scott Rutherford and Ed Daniels, members of the VVRP board of directors. The team consisted of eight veterans, the spouse of one veteran, and Harold Mondol, who was along to produce a documentary film of our journey. We were given helpful information about every aspect of our trip. We also shared with one another our reasons for returning and our hopes, expectations, and concerns. At the conclusion of the team training, we had formed a close-knit and mutually supportive community that assured we would realize to the utmost the benefits of the life-changing journey (of healing and reconciliation) on which we were embarking.

Diary Notes from the Trip

Monday, March 30: We wrapped up three days of training this morning and are now preparing to enjoy a send-off dinner at King Strong's home and then on to San Francisco International Airport for a 1:20 a.m. flight to Hong Kong. I am feeling a little apprehensive, but am looking forward to the trip and the mission we are on. I am concerned about Mom, as she is in the hospital and weak.

11:45 p.m. We are now sitting at the San Francisco International airport ready to leave for Hong Kong. We had really good food and drinks at King Strong's home before departing for the airport.

Wednesday, April 1: We arrived in Hanoi around 10:30 a.m. I was amazed at the improvements that had been made to Noi Bai Airport since I had last visited Hanoi in 1998. After arriving at the Freedom Hotel, where we will be staying until Saturday, we went to a bank to exchange U.S. dollars for Vietnamese currency, the Dong. We then went to meet with an official of the Ministry of Labor, Invalids, and Social Affairs (MOLISA). We had a very cordial meeting. She talked a lot about Agent Orange and the long-term effects the chemical defoliant has had on the

Vietnamese population. Later, we had a team meeting and then went out for dinner.

Thursday, April 2: Eight of us from the team toured around Hanoi today. We visited the War Museum, the Hanoi Hilton prison, and had a great lunch at a restaurant by Hoan Kiem Lake. It rained most of the day and is cool.

VVRP Team XXIV met with Vietnamese officials while in Hanoi.

Friday, April 3: This morning we traveled to the Village of Friendship, a place for children of veterans who suffer from the effects of Agent Orange. We visited classrooms while school was in session. The children seemed to enjoy our presence and the goodies we had for them. The village offers therapeutic help for mentally and physically disabled children as well as their educational training and medical care. We also visited a new building for adults who suffer the consequences of war.

In the afternoon, after having lunch at the Season's, we visited a museum. Following that visit, we traveled to the Hanoi Hilton Hotel to meet Lieutenant General Dong Sy Nguyen, who engineered the Ho Chi Minh Trail. He said, "Your humanitarian aid work helps bring people closer and any help is appreciated." He thanked us very much for coming to Vietnam. He said, "When we meet in a peaceful spot like this, we are the most happiest." In the evening, several of us went to the Kangaroo Café and had a few beers. Bai Hanoi beer tasted pretty good after a long day touring the city. We later had dinner.

Saturday, April 4: This morning we are flying to Hue on Vietnam Airlines. Arriving in Hue, we checked into the Asia Hotel near the Perfume River. The rest of the day was spent relaxing and having dinner at Ushi's Restaurant, located across the street from the hotel.

Sunday, April 5: The day started out well with breakfast on the top floor of the Asia Hotel. Following a team meeting, we toured and shopped the city. We took a team picture crossing the Perfume River. We toured around Hue on cyclos. We returned to Ushi's later in the morning. I learned that Ushi was seven years old and living in Hue with her family during the Tet Offensive in 1968. In the afternoon, we

went to the Mandarin Café, where we met Mr. Cu. He had some pictures of the street where his café is located and what it looked like following Tet 1968, and what the street looked like in 2001. Tonight, we are having a team dinner at Ushi's.

Vietnamese construction crew and VVRP Team.

Monday, April 6: Today, we traveled to A Luoi. I was surprised by the mountainous, rough terrain along the highway going to A Luoi. When we arrived in A Luoi, we met with Vietnamese officials, who welcomed us to A Luoi and thanked us for coming to help on the school project. Following the meeting, we went to the school project and met the construction crew, teachers, and children. The children were very friendly. We then went to a local café for lunch. The food was very Vietnamese and did not taste very good. They leave the bones in the meats (chicken, pork and beef). In the chicken, there was a cooked claw. Following dinner, we came to the hotel, where we will be staying for the next two weeks. We spent the afternoon shopping and resting.

While shopping, as we walked through the market, an elderly Vietnamese woman lightly kicked me as she lay on a bench, trying to take a nap. I guess I somehow disturbed her while she was trying to rest. Our group gathered at six for dinner, which was much better than lunch. After dinner, when we arrived back at our rooms, the lights were out, so am writing this by candlelight and flashlight. The weather is very cool with a light mist. I am looking forward to tomorrow and working on the school project.

Tuesday April 7: Today started early. The lights came on again at about 1 a.m. After breakfast, we stopped to purchase our lunch. We arrived at the school job site around 8:30 a.m. The children were happy to see us! It is rather cool for this time of year. The mountains in the distance have a lot of fog and mist surrounding them. Hamburger Hill is visible in the far distance.

Author shoveling sand through a screen, preparing it for the concrete mixer.

My main job today was shoveling sand through a screen to prepare it for the concrete mixer. Following lunch and a one and one-half hour break, so that the children could rest, we returned to the school and finished the day out at around

2:30 p.m. We then came back to the guest house where we are staying and cleaned up. We then went to visit the kindergarten school VVRP completed two years ago. The children sang and performed for us, which was very touching. We then came back to the guest house and had dinner, followed by a trip to get some ice cream.

Wednesday, April 8: The day once again started early as we had breakfast at 7:00 a.m. and then left at 7:30 a.m. for the work site. The weather is still cloudy and cool. At the work site, I shoveled more sand and enjoyed the beautiful scenery and hearing children laughing and playing.

After lunch, we came back to the guest house where we are staying. About thirty minutes later, we departed on a trip to a resort area west of A Luoi. There were some nice homes on stilts along the way. Some of the homes had hunter green roofs and, of course, satellite TV. We relaxed by a mountain stream. The mountains were very beautiful to look at.

We then came back to our guest house, showered, and relaxed for the rest of the day. Following dinner, we were invited into the home of the people who run the restaurant next to the guest house. They have a very nice home by Vietnamese standards. We listened to a CD that team member Bud had brought along. We sang along with the music and had a great time!

Thursday, April 9: This morning, we left for the work site early, 7:30 a.m., to beat the heat. By 9:00 a.m., it was already getting hot. I shoveled more sand and helped carry brick. We finished the brick pile around 10:00 a.m. and then came back to the guest house. When we arrived, the electricity was out for the second time since we arrived here. So far, working on the school project has been healing for me.

This afternoon, we visited a veterans' cemetery here in A Luoi. We stopped at a flower shop on the way and purchased a beautiful wreath, which stated VVRP TEAM XXIV A Ngo "With Honor." Later in the afternoon, a twelve-year-old-girl was presented a new bike. VVRP Team XXII had purchased her a bike and it was later stolen. It was very pleasing to see the expression on her face when the new bike was brought out for her.

So far, this has been a very positive experience. Coming back after forty-one years to help rebuild has made me feel good. Seeing the school that was completed two years ago and witnessing the school children so bright-eyed and happy was wonderful!

Friday, April 10: Friday was a short workday. We got to the work site about 8:00 a.m. and worked until 10:00 a.m. By then, it was really getting warm. We packed up and came back to Hue. Friday evening, Ushi cooked a nice Mexican-flavored dinner for the group.

Saturday, April 11: Today, we left around 8:00 a.m. for Hoi An. Bud knows a family who lives there. Bruce, Dan, Jill, Bud, and I went on the trip. We went over the Hai Van Pass before arriving in Danang. We arrived in Hoi An, which is south of Danang, and found a place to have lunch and do some shopping. Following that, we went to a fancy hotel where Bud's friend worked. It was a very beautiful setting. We then traveled to Bud's friend's home for a short visit and some green tea. Following the visit, we headed back to Hue, arriving at 6:00 p.m. Later in the evening, the group went out for dinner.

Easter Sunday, April 12: Today we slept in until 8:00 a.m. At 10:00 a.m., my guide, driver, Dan, Dave, Harold, and I traveled to Thon La Chu, a village near Hue, where my unit was ambushed on February 13, 1968, during the Tet Offensive. I had some mixed emotions about being there, but overall, am glad that I went. We visited with some of the locals who were there during Tet and learned some of the history during that time period. There was a hospital there that the Viet Cong and NVA used. The village didn't look the same as forty-one years ago.

Monday, April 13: This morning, things started off with the electricity at the hotel going out. Dave was stranded in the elevator just before it reached ground floor. He had to be rescued. We traveled north to Quang Tri and then on to Dong Ha. From there, we traveled to the DMZ area and then north to the Vinh Moc Tunnels. From the tunnels, we traveled back toward Dong Ha along the coast, stopping to have lunch along the way.

On the way back to A Luoi traveling along Route 9, we had a flat tire on the bus and were delayed for one and one-half hours while the tire was being repaired. Continuing on, we stopped for a group picture by the Rockpile. We then traveled across the Dakrong Bridge and onto the Ho Chi Minh Highway for a harrowing ride through the mountains on our way back to A Luoi for dinner, showers, and bed.

Tuesday, April 14: Today, the day started early, coffee at 6 a.m. and breakfast at 6:30 a.m. After stopping to purchase some food and water, we went to the work site. It had rained since we were there last Friday. We carried brick inside the classrooms. It is very hot and humid today, just as I remembered Vietnam during my tour of duty.

The VVRP Team XXIV wheel barrowed and hand carried this huge pile of bricks inside the school. Pictured above is team member Dan Albrecht.

After lunch at the restaurant by the guest house, I took a nap, as it rained a downpour for an hour or so. Later in the afternoon, I happened to be in the restaurant when Mark, a VVRP team member gave a bike to a young woman who worked there. She was a very happy girl! I am thinking about buying a bike for her family also, as they have no transportation. Her father passed away a number of years ago.

Wednesday, April 15: Today, we went back to the job site around 8:00 a.m. and worked until 10:00 a.m., as it was humid and getting very hot. I shoveled more sand. I also found a bamboo stick to take with me for my upcoming Hamburger Hill climb. We came back to the guest house for lunch. Ushi came to pick up my roomie, Bud, who is going to go home. John Ward will be my roommate for the next two nights.

New A Ngo Commune kindergarten school under construction.

Today is the day that we will give two bikes to a family who had no bikes, except for the one young woman who Mark had given a bike to yesterday. At the team meeting last night, Smitty and I, with the help of Dan, Jill, and Bruce, decided to purchase two more bikes for the family.

Around noon, Tuan, our tour guide, and I went to the bike store and picked out two bikes, one green and one blue.

It was arranged to bring the family in from the countryside around 3:00 p.m. At 2:00 p.m., Tuan, Smitty, and I picked up the bikes and took them to the restaurant. The family of the young woman who worked at the restaurant arrived at 3:15 p.m. Besides the oldest daughter, who had received a bike the day before, there was the mother, and the rest of the family, a fourteen-year-old girl, a seventeen-year-old boy, a ten-year-old boy, and an eight-year-old girl. When the family saw the bikes, they were very happy. There was a lot of picture-taking with many happy smiles! I was feeling this is what we also came for, to make a difference in the life of a family. Since the father had died years earlier, they were very poor and had to walk everywhere. It made me very happy (and emotional) to be a part of giving the bikes to the family. It has been a good day in Vietnam. Tomorrow morning, several of us on the team will climb Hamburger Hill.

Thursday, April 16: Today, we started early as today is the day that we will climb Hamburger Hill. Six of us, Dan, Dave, John, two Vietnamese guides, and I, boarded the bus around 7:30 a.m. for the trip up to the base of the mountain. We slowly wound our way up toward Hamburger Hill, passing through many small villages. We stopped at one point along the way while a Vietnamese Army lieutenant was summoned to travel along with us. The lieutenant was not very sociable. We continued on up the winding narrow road toward the mountain. When we got close to the mountain, we ran into some road construction and had to park the bus.

From there, we started the hike up to the top of the mountain. Along the path, we encountered several steep concrete steps to climb. There was steady conversation along the way. We encountered construction workers along the way, building the road to the top. When we arrived near the top of the mountain, we discovered they were building a shrine. From there, we walked a little further, and the trail turned into a narrow jungle path. It reminded me of being back out on patrol hunting "Charlie" (the Viet Cong). It was like the eerie feeling I had in the jungle during the war.

We then took a path to the site of a helicopter crash. I left a small American flag in memory of those who died during the war. After about a half-hour, we returned to the area where they were building the shrine. We then started down the mountain. About halfway down, it started to thunder, lightning, and rain. By the time we reached the bus, it was pouring rain. Because there was no place to turn the bus around, we started backing up the road. After awhile, the bus became stuck in the mud. We all jumped out of the bus and threw rocks in the road for traction. We then helped push the bus up the hill. After we got going again, we finally found a place to turn around. I was having my doubts if we were going to make it out of there. It rained the rest of the way back to the guest house, but we are safely back.

At 4:00 p.m., the team gathered and we went back to the school for dinner. The school board was hosting an appreciation dinner for the team. When we arrived at the school, they had laid out a huge dinner on the floor in one of the classrooms. There was sticky rice in banana peel, beef, chicken, fish, and other authentic Vietnamese food.

Kindergarten children and teachers at A Ngo Commune school.

Following dinner, there was singing, dancing, and a lot of laughter. One elderly Vietnamese man played a homemade flute. Many native children came and crowded in the door to see what was going on in the classroom. After some picture-taking and saying our farewells, we headed back to the guest house to await the arrival of the teachers for more food, drink, singing, clapping, and laughter. It had been a good day.

Friday, April 17: Following breakfast, the team went back out to the school to mingle around the project site and say good-bye to the children and teachers. We then went back to the restaurant by the guest house to clean up and wait the arrival of the school project construction workers. We had a nice dinner with the workers, making many toasts. Following dinner, we packed up and left for Hue. We arrived in mid-afternoon. That evening, Ushi cooked an American dinner for our last VVRP team meal. I spent the next couple of days in Hue, sightseeing and gift shopping. Dave and I were roommates for the remainder of the trip.

Saturday, April 18: After enjoying a hearty breakfast at the Asian Hotel, I walked down the street from the hotel to do some shopping. While I paused in front of a store, a Vietnamese man on a motorbike approached me and suggested that he knew me. I was somewhat taken aback, but listened to what he had to say. He invited me to jump on his motorbike and go have coffee at a place near the Perfume River. I hesitated for a moment, but decided to take him up on his offer, as he looked trustworthy.

After climbing on the motorbike, we took off and I begin to have doubts about this venture. I didn't know for sure where he was taking me. For all I knew, he could be taking me anywhere to be mugged or worse. All of a sudden, I wanted off the bike, but he never slowed down until we came to a café by the river. We had coffee and I learned that he offered bike tours around Hue. I thought it would be fun to tour the city on a motorbike, so I paid him and off we went.

Following the tour, he offered to have me come to his house for dinner the next day. I thought that was kind of odd, but I assumed that he was just being friendly. I politely declined his offer. I found out later from Ushi that by having dinner at his house, he was setting me up for a shakedown by playing on my sympathy to help him and his family financially.

Sunday, April 19: Today was my last full day in Hue. Tomorrow Dave and I will be flying back to Hanoi. Smitty offered to take me along with his Vietnamese friends to a hot springs spa about forty-five minutes northwest of Hue. I decided this would be a good way to spend the day, so I accepted the offer. Arriving at the hot springs spa park, I was amazed at how nicely the area had been developed. Even though it was a very warm day, we had an enjoyable time.

Monday, April 20: Today, we are flying back to Hanoi. I am starting to get anxious to go home. Since Ushi was going to Danang to do some shopping and would be going right by the airport, Dave, Charlie Wishart—President of the Board of Directors of VVRP—and I hitched a ride to the airport with her. We arrived in Hanoi in mid-afternoon and went to the Freedom Hotel. We later had dinner together.

Tuesday, April 21: Today was my last full day in Vietnam. At the Kangaroo Café, I was able to make arrangements to once again visit the Birla Children's Village. In the morning, one of the young women who worked at the café took me shopping for school supplies and goodies for the village. It was a fun trip. Around 4:00 p.m. my translator and driver picked me up in front of the hotel. We traveled south for about thirty minutes through heavy traffic to get to the orphanage.

Author poses with some of the children at the Birla Children's Village.

The Hanoi traffic is just amazing. Motorbikes, cars, buses all coming at each other, yet they seem to miss one another and no one shows anger, they just give, slow down for the next guy, and go on. There is honking everywhere in the streets. When we arrived at the village, I was warmly greeted by the director, Chu Dinh Diep. After a short visit, we took a tour of the village, meeting some of the children and their housemothers. The children seemed genuinely curious about my presence in their midst. They were very friendly and happy when the goodies I had brought along were given out. At the end of my visit, about twenty children gathered together for a picture with me. I arrived back at the hotel around 6:00 p.m. and was greeted by Dave and Charlie. We later went the Kangaroo Café for dinner.

Wednesday, April 22: Today was my last day in Vietnam. We just arrived in Hong Kong from Hanoi a short while ago and am now sitting on the plane ready to fly to San Francisco. I am having a lot of emotions about leaving. I just glanced up and saw a young stewardess approaching my seat with a look of concern on her face. She asked, "Are you all right?" My emotions must have been showing. I replied, "I'm okay." In reality, I had tears in my eyes and was feeling as though I was leaving a part of myself behind. So many in Vietnam have so little, yet they seem happy and are a determined people. (Note: End of diary.)

As a young twenty-year-old soldier in 1968, I couldn't wait to get out of Vietnam. Traveling back forty-two years later, I wasn't sure I was ready to leave. In the weeks and months since my return, I've been able to reflect on the many varied sights and sounds and the surging feelings I felt in my often profoundly moving daily encounters working and socializing with the Vietnamese people and my fellow vets on the trip.

As I relive the still-fresh and vivid experiences of the three-week trip now that I'm back in my ordinary life here in Kansas, I've become conscious of a new awareness that has gradually taken root in my daily outlook on life that leaves me with a renewed sense of the preciousness of my life and my wish to turn my efforts toward acts that build and create and affirm.

Since my return, I'm also more conscious of my commitments and values as my new awareness of possibilities deepens into a conviction that we can, and even must, turn something as negative as war's obscene, seemingly never-ending suffering into something positive and constructive. I realize that it is important that I pass my new sense of possibilities along to others who can also benefit from what I've learned.

HEALING WALL Author poses at newly constructed A Ngo Commune kindergarten school.

I feel like I have come full-circle with my Vietnam experience, from surviving and witnessing death and destruction during the war, to coming back and being part of a rebuilding effort. The journey back with Veterans Vietnam Restoration Project was very healing. It has given me a new sense of peace deep within my soul. Taking action can be a very powerful thing. Being part of something far bigger than yourself is very rewarding.

Tran - Hung - Dao st   TET 1968

TRAN-HUNG-DAO st. HUE-VN
Tet - 2001

Photo courtesy of Mr Cu

For more information about joining a VVRP team or to make a tax deductible contribution to help fund future VVRP projects, visit the website at www.vvrp.org.

Citation

BY DIRECTION OF THE PRESIDENT
THE AIR MEDAL

IS PRESENTED TO

SPECIALIST FOUR E-4 LEONARD W. PURINTON US55984209

UNITED STATES ARMY

For distinguishing himself by meritorious achievement while participating in sustained aerial flight in support of combat ground forces of the Republic of Vietnam during the period

APRIL 1967 TO APRIL 1968

During this time he actively participated in more than twenty-five aerial missions over hostile territory in support of counterinsurgency operations. During all of these missions he displayed the highest order of air discipline and acted in accordance with the best traditions of the service. By his determination to accomplish his mission in spite of the hazards inherent in repeated aerial flights over hostile territory and by his outstanding degree of professionalism and devotion to duty, he has brought credit upon himself, his organization, and the military service.

Citation

BY DIRECTION OF THE SECRETARY OF THE ARMY
THE ARMY COMMENDATION MEDAL

IS PRESENTED TO

SPECIALIST FOUR E-4 LEONARD W. PURINTUM US55598209

UNITED STATES ARMY

For the performance of exceptionally meritorious service in support of the United States objectives in the counterinsurgency effort in the Republic of Vietnam during the period

APRIL 1967 TO APRIL 1968

Through his outstanding professional competence and devotion to duty he consistently obtained superior results. Working long and arduous hours, he set an example that inspired his associates to strive for maximum achievement. The loyalty, initiative and will to succeed that he demonstrated at all times materially contributed to the successful accomplishment of the mission of this command. His performance was in the best traditions of the United States Army and reflects great credit upon himself and the military service.

END NOTES

1. The History Place www.historyplace.com/unitedstates/viet/index-1965. html

2. Trivia-Library.com www.trivia-library.com/.../okinawa-islands-location-history-size-population-and-government.htm

3. Cavalry Outpost Publications www.first-team.us/journals/3rd _bde/3b_ ndx.html

4. U S Centennial of Flight Commission – Pamela Feltus www.centennial-offlight.gov/essay/Air-Power/.../AP37.htm

5. Setting the conditions of War Crimes by Marjorie Cohn

   www.thirdworldtraveler.com/war-crimes/SetConditions-WarCrimes.html

6. Enemy Body Counts Revived By: Bradley Graham

   Washington Post Staff Writer Monday, October 24, 2005: A01

   www.washingtonpost.com.>World>MiddleEast>Iraq

7. Charles Hirschman et al.; Vietnamese Casualties During the American War: A New Estimate, Population and Development Review, Vol.21, No 4. (Dec., 1995),pp. 783-812.

8. History.com www.history.com/this-day.../congressman-m-16-is-defective

9. en.wikipedia.org/wiki/Punji_stick

10. http://www.answers.com/topic/air-assault

11. Vietnam Veterans Terminology and Slang

Dictionary of Vietnam War edited by James S. Olson

Greenwood Press, Inc.; New York, 1988

12. Reprinted with the permission of the Chippewa Herald, Chippewa, WI and Lee Enterprises By: Staff Reporter: Mark Gunderman

13. en.wikipedia.org/wiki/William_D_Port

14. U S Army of Military History.com

15. Vietnam.usembassy.gov>...>US-Vietnam Relations

Page numbers in italics represent photographs.

229

ABOUT THE AUTHOR

Wayne Purinton was born in 1947 and raised on a farm near Collyer, Kansas. He graduated from Trego Community High School, WaKeeney, Kansas, in 1965. He volunteered for the draft a year after high school. After Vietnam, he graduated from Dodge City Community College, Dodge City, Kansas, in 1972. He farmed for 25 years, before retiring in 1998. Wayne married Sandy Berends in 1972. They have three children, Troy, Gina, and Royce.

He was diagnosed with Post-Traumatic Stress Disorder in 1997, due to his combat experiences in the Vietnam War from 1967-1968. His parents had saved letters he wrote home from Vietnam. They were discovered in his parent's closet in June 2000. The letters sparked an interest in writing a book about his war experiences, which would include the letters home.